The Warric
Making Your Lif

To Andrew —

May you never walk
away from the Warrior
lifestyle.

Bohdi Sanders

The Warrior Lifestyle
Making Your Life Extraordinary

Bohdi Sanders, PhD

First Edition

(Volume Three of the Warrior Wisdom Series)
Published by Kaizen Quest Publishing

Printed in the United States of America

Library of Congress Cataloging-in-Publication Data
Sanders, Bohdi, 1962-
The Warrior Lifestyle: Making Your Life Extraordinary

ISBN – 978-1-937884-02-4

1. Martial Arts. 2. Self-Help. 3. Philosophy. I. Title

Acknowledgements

This book is dedicated to the true warriors in this world. May you continue to live with honor and find victory over your enemies - both external and internal.

I want to thank my wife Tracey for her continued support and encouragement during the many long hours which I spend in my office writing. None of the *Warrior Wisdom* books would have come to fruition without her continued support.

I also want to thank all of the people who so kindly supported my efforts in writing this book.

Loren W. Christensen
Kevin Brett
Alain Burrese
F. J. Chu
Wim Demeere
Kris Wilder

And a special thank you to my friend Charlie Ward who left this world much too soon, and who supported my writing continuously during his lifetime. He told me many times he considered me to be like a brother to him. You are missed my friend.

Dr. Charlie Ward

About the Author

Bohdi Sanders is a lifelong student of wisdom literature, the healing arts, and the martial arts. His studies led him to explore the wisdom behind natural health, naturopathy, herbs, Reiki, Qigong, meditation and the power of the mind to heal the body and to make positive changes in one's life. These explorations led to him earning doctorate degrees in naturopathy and in natural health.

Dr. Sanders is also a Certified Personal Fitness Trainer, a Certified Specialist in Martial Arts Conditioning, a Certified Reiki Master, and a Certified Master of G-Jo Acupressure. He holds a black belt in Shotokan Karate and has studied various other martial arts for over 30 years. He has worked with young people for over 20 years and is endorsed to teach in five different subject areas. He is the author of:

- *Warrior Wisdom: Ageless Wisdom for the Modern Warrior*
- *Warrior Wisdom: The Heart and Soul of Bushido*
- *The Warrior Lifestyle: Making Your Life Extraordinary*
- *The Secrets of Worldly Wisdom*
- *Secrets of the Soul*
- *Wisdom of the Elders*
- *Modern Bushido: Living a Life of Excellence*

Dr. Sanders' books have received high praise and have won several national awards, including:

- The Indie Excellence Book Awards: 1st Place Winner 2010
- USA Book News Best Books of 2010: 1st Place Winner 2010
- IIMAA: Best Martial Arts Book of the Year 2011
- USA Martial Arts HOF: Literary Man of the Year 2011
- U. S. Martial Artist Association: Inspiration of the Year 2011
- U. S. Martial Arts Hall of Fame: Author of the Year 2011

www.TheWisdomWarrior.com

Endorsements for The Warrior Lifestyle

Dr. Bohdi Sanders has rendered society a great service with *The Warrior Lifestyle*. He has collected, preserved, explained and shared timeless wisdom with the next generation. The primary duty and privilege of the elders of any culture is to educate and prepare the next generation of citizens and warriors. *The Warrior Lifestyle* does this.

Warriors exist so that citizens may exist, however do not be misled by the title. *The Warrior Lifestyle* applies to each of us. The truths that Dr. Sanders has captured are a timeless snapshot of the cherished warrior creed that we must wholly embrace to survive and prosper in our time. Our children desperately need this wisdom and these lessons so that they are enlightened and strengthened for their roles as our future leaders. Without it their education is incomplete.

In an age where murky relativism obscures clarity of vision and action, *The Warrior Lifestyle*, pierces the fog with a clear framework of definitive and actionable principles. These are the principles of honor, courage, service and compassion that have guided and defined the most honored intellects in human history. *The Warrior Lifestyle* skillfully integrates the collective wisdom of Buddha, Confucius, Jesus, Seneca, Churchill, Aesop, Sun Tzu, Gandhi, Lao Tzu, Thomas Paine, George Washington and countless other greats. Dr. Sanders has assembled this treasure trove of ageless wisdom to provide us with a moral compass for conscience, conduct and purpose that we can easily apply to our daily life.

Read it. Internalize it. Live it.

Kevin Brett

CEO, Kevin Brett Studios, Inc.
Author of: The Way of the Martial Artist: Achieving Success in Martial Arts and in Life!

Endorsements for The Warrior Lifestyle

The Warrior Lifestyle is the welcome third installment of the *Warrior Wisdom* series by Dr. Bohdi Sanders. In my opinion, Dr. Sanders' book could easily be titled Worldly Wisdom due to the vast spectrum of individuals quoted and the profound advice on how to live life not only as a warrior, but as a person of honor, integrity, and moral rightness, attributes that Sanders believes a warrior must possess, and something I agree with him on wholeheartedly. If the passages are meditated upon, one will find this a journal of self-discovery and personal enlightenment. I'm not suggesting you will find Nirvana in a book, but rather if contemplated upon you will find numerous circumstances and situations where the advice in this text can help you live a more fulfilling life.

The Warrior Lifestyle connects the martial way with a larger perspective, merging philosophies from Sun Tzu to Bruce Lee, Aristotle to Winston Churchill, Confucius to Douglas MacArthur, Lao Tzu and Jesus to Mark Twain and Benjamin Franklin. It contains wisdom from modern day self-defense authors such as Loren Christensen as well as from the classic texts such as Miyamoto Musashi's *Book of Five Rings*.

In fact, it is one of Musashi's quotes which is my favorite from the book, "As a human being one should train one's mind and one's ability to the fullest." Dr. Sanders comments on this quote that the warrior must do whatever he does 100%, whether it is gardening or honing his martial arts skills. He further adds the important of balance, and states that you must train your mind, body, and spirit to the fullest, but make sure to maintain a sense of balance. The advice provided in the *Warrior Wisdom* series will help one forge their character into that of a warrior, one who trains body, mind, and spirit to the fullest while maintaining balance, and that is the key to not only warrior wisdom, but worldly wisdom. If you want to discover your warrior's edge, read this book.

Alain B. Burrese, J.D.

Author of: *Hard-Won Wisdom from the School of Hard Knocks*, and the DVD's: *Hapkido Hoshinsul, Hapkido Cane, Streetfighting Essentials*, and the *Lock On: Joint Locking Essentials* series.

Endorsements for The Warrior Lifestyle

The *Warrior Wisdom* books, by Dr. Bohdi Sanders, are books that every single martial artist should have in their personal library. They should be read, and re-read, regularly through the years ahead – and the knowledge within those pages should be shared with everyone.

As a professional martial arts instructor, and a retired professional NHB fighter myself, I find myself disappointed in the lack of traditional martial arts values that I sometimes see in the martial arts world, and the competitive MMA scene today. Those who would call themselves warriors should have Dr. Sanders' books as required reading material, to help teach them and remind them of what it really means to be a warrior, and what it means to truly embrace the warrior lifestyle.

I am honored to call Dr. Sanders my friend, and I am very proud to have him as a professional colleague and fellow warrior! I cannot recommend his books highly enough! Not just for modern martial artists, warriors, and fighters – but for everyone. Dr. Sanders' writings provide his readers with an accurate understanding and appreciation of the true Martial Spirit, and the art of "Right Living" as a warrior.

Dr. Charles Ward, Ph.D./Ma.D.Sc, CSCS

Professor/Chief Master Instructor Trainer
USA Martial Arts Hall of Fame Member
Bare-Knuckle Freestyle NHB World Champion-Retired
United States Muay Thai Association-Arizona State Director
Ward's Living Weapon Fight Science

Endorsements for The Warrior Lifestyle

In this book, Dr. Bohdi Sanders collects wisdom from all ages and cultures, from 13th century Zen masters and philosophers to ancient Greece, and from world leaders to modern day warriors. All of these extraordinary men have left us wisdom that can teach us important life lessons, lessons just as applicable today as they were thousands of years ago.

But a quote in and of itself is often useless without the proper context, a context that helps you understand the deeper meaning and nuances that are usually hidden at first. This is exactly what Bohdi Sanders brings to this book. He gives you his insights to help you contemplate and grasp the wisdom contained in the quotes he has included in *The Warrior Lifestyle.*

You'll not only find new understanding through his commentaries, but more importantly, you will also learn real-life-applicable knowledge throughout the many pages of this book. I highly recommend *The Warrior Lifestyle.*

Wim Demeere

Martial Artist and Black Belt
He teaches his knowledge worldwide in both seminars and through his numerous books and instructional DVDs. You can visit his website at: www.wimdemeere.com or read and participate on his blog at www.wimsblog.com.

Endorsements for The Warrior Lifestyle

Can wisdom be taught? Bohdi Sanders' latest volume contains a collection of aphorism-inspired observations about cultivating the warrior mentality. If a picture is equal to a thousand words, then Dr. Sanders has provided us with 165 verbal images of how to follow the Martial Way. Drawing upon an eclectic list of Eastern and Western sources from antiquity to the modern day, the author repeatedly counsels aspiring martial artists to do two things: first, always do what is just and true; second, always train as if it really matters. As Marcus Aurelius said, "Do every act of your life as if it were your last."

Dr. Sanders is dedicated with following the path of the warrior. One can debate whether warrior wisdom can really be taught, but Dr. Sanders shows us that it certainly can be nurtured and reinforced. Reserve a place on your bookshelf for this volume and turn to it for flashes of insight and inspiration. As for me, I am partial to Cervantes' observation that "proverbs are short sentences drawn from long experience."

F. J. Chu

Author of: *The Martial Way and Its Virtues*

Endorsements for The Warrior Lifestyle

Dr. Bohdi Sanders brings the wisdom of multiple disciplines together in *The Warrior Lifestyle*. Bringing east and west, and different walks of life together, Dr. Sanders teases out the hard questions, the paths of self betterment and insightful observations. This book will go on your book shelf, but will not rest there as you will go back to it again and again for inspiration.

Kris Wilder

Martial Artist and 5th Dan Black Belt
Author of: *The Way of Sanchin Kata* and co-author of: *The Way of Kata, The Way to Black Belt* and *The Little Black Book of Violence*.

Foreword

There is an image on my coffee cup of John Wayne, complete with cowboy hat, weathered face, and a squint of the eyes that conveys compassion, understanding, and you mess with me and I will mess with your face. On the other side of the cup, there is a quote from one of Wayne's movies; "A man's got to have a code, a creed to live by."

As a guy who has been kicking, punching, and grappling in the martial arts since 1965, I understand this totally; that is, I do *now*. In my early years, my instruction was just on fighting. There was no mention of a code, ethics, morals or honorable warriorhood. Even if there had been, I am not sure how receptive I would have been to the subject. During those early years, I just wanted to learn how to thump, beat, and crush; I just wanted to fill my container of whoop ass.

Once I got it nearly full, (it's never complete filled, as there is always something to learn), I went on to open that can and open it a lot. I like to think I was never the aggressor, but there were nonetheless times when I hurt people unnecessarily. I "over defended" myself, if you will.

I was 19 years old the first time. The assailant was a big and nasty drunk, and although I had never seen him before, he chose me to attack out of all the other teens at the burger joint. I managed to block his onslaught and then countered with a kick to his larynx, sending him sprawling across the windshield of a Volkswagen Bug. That would have likely ended it, but I continued to "defend myself" with a rainstorm of punches on the hapless guy, all the while the couple inside the little car held each other and screamed in terror. Thirty minutes later, I was sitting in jail as my assailant was getting his throat worked on in the emergency room.

Could I have handled the situation with greater control of the attacker and myself? Oh, yes, and by doing so, I wouldn't have hurt the man so badly, and I wouldn't have had the hassle and embarrassment of iron-bar incarceration, (I served one hour).

At that stage in my life, I hadn't learned what John Wayne called, "A code, a creed to live by," nor even heard of Sun Tzu and his quotation, "Rage and resentment lead to rash action," that Dr. Bohdi Sanders discusses so well in this book. All I had learned was how to open that can of you-know-what.

Three years later, I was working as a military policeman in Saigon and was involved in a large raid of an off-limits area in which there were dozens of American GI's. At one point during one of many melees, I was scuffling with a Marine and having a difficult time due to his great strength. When I pushed him against a cyclone fence, he used it to bounce back, his arms reaching out for me. I was ready though, with a burst of temper and a hard cross punch into his chest, which dropped him instantly and launched his heart into cardiac arrest.

He lay on the street limp and in and out of consciousness for several minutes before an ambulance whisked him away to the hospital where doctors were uncertain whether he would survive. It was a long night waiting for word on his prognosis, waiting to hear if the young Marine would die and I would spend many years doing hard time in a military prison. Thankfully, he lived.

I thought of this incident when I read Dr. Sanders' discussion of the Chinese Maxim, "The more quickly brought to anger, the more quickly brought to death." Most often, people discuss this as the one who gets angry is the one who dies, but in my clash with the Marine, it was my anger that nearly caused his death.

There would be many other similar incidents over the years (the interested reader will find an analysis of these in my book *Crouching Tiger*) until I finally had an epiphany; *Hurting people and responding to violent situations like a caveman wasn't why I trained, nor was it the kind of person I wanted to be.* (Epiphanies are often simple and leave you wondering why it took you so long to see the light.)

Because I chose a career in law enforcement that brought me face-to-face with violence on almost a daily basis, and because other police officers, my superiors, the public, and the media, scrutinized my every action, I began a course of self-analyzing and self-critiquing. I initially did this out of a desire for self-preservation – I didn't want to be fired or sued. But as time passed, as my years in the martial arts accumulated, as I matured to see that the fighting arts are so much more than just opening that can, my self-analysis took on the form of wanting to do the right thing. I wanted to, "Shun any action that will diminish honor," a quotation by Tiruvalluvar, that Dr. Sanders discusses so wisely.

After every violent situation, I would ask myself such questions as; how could I have done a better job? How did my actions help diffuse the situation? How did they amplify it? How do I feel as a person now? How do I feel as a warrior now?

If I didn't handle a situation well, I tried to understand why. Did I lose my temper? If so, why? Did I abuse my power? If so, why? Did I hurt the person unnecessarily? If so, why? How did my improper actions make me feel as a person, and how did they affect my art, my job, my family, and my students? In short, I was trying to understand and ultimately follow the truest and best path. In short, I was just trying to do on my own what Dr. Sanders has done for all of us with his very insightful selection of relevant quotes combined with his marvelous interpretation of each and every one of those quotes in his *Warrior Wisdom* series.

I'm reminded of that scene in the movie *The Wedding Singer* when the bride-to-be tells Adam Sandler's character the day after she had stood him up at the altar, "I never wanted to marry you." Sandler's character responds, "Jeeze, you know, that information might have been a little more useful to me yesterday."

Well, Bohdi, I wish you had written these books 40 years ago before I got into all that trouble. *The Warrior Lifestyle*, like all of Dr. Sanders' books in this series, is a wonderful guide to living your life ethically, morally, compassionately, wisely, and exemplarily. Oh, I forgot one. It will keep you out of trouble too.

There are many ways to read this book. Here is one; read just one *Warrior Wisdom* quote a day and roll its surface meaning around in your mind for a while to understand its immediate gist, then dig down a layer and think about what you find there. Keep going deeper and deeper until you thoroughly understand how the wisdom quotation relates to new events of the day, to people with whom you associate, and to you and your life experiences.

Although not everyone agrees on the definition of a warrior, one that I like and is hard to dispute is this: *A warrior does what needs to be done.* Reading, contemplating and applying the information in *The Warrior Lifestyle* and all the other volumes in the *Warrior Wisdom* series, will provide you with a code and creed to live by as you endeavor to do the right thing.

Loren W. Christensen

Author of: *Fighter's Fact Book, Fighter's Fact Book 2, Solo Training, Solo Training 2, Speed Training, Fighting Power, The Fighter's Body*; and a whole heck of a lot more. Loren can be reached via his website: www.lwcbooks.com

Introduction

The Warrior Lifestyle is the third book in the *Warrior Wisdom* series, and continues to offer the reader insight into the warrior lifestyle. The warrior lifestyle is not what most people seem to think it is; it is a lifestyle based on the perfection of character, and not based on violence. To many people, the mental image that they visualize when they think of a warrior is that of a brute programmed for war. They picture a killing machine whose only concern is war – Rambo with no personal compass.

This is a common misconception where the true warrior is concerned. While the main definition of the warrior found in most dictionaries is, "Somebody who takes part in or has experience in warfare." This definition is not the one that should be used to define the true warrior, and is not an accurate definition for the warrior lifestyle. A better definition for a warrior is, "Somebody who takes part in a struggle or conflict." The true warrior is engaged in a struggle and it is a daily fight. His battle is not necessarily on the battlefield, but rather a personal battle to perfect his character and to become a man of excellence in every area of his life.

The relentless enemy that he must face is that of his base nature. He battles this enemy daily, constantly repelling the temptation to lower his personal standards which he has decided to make an integral part of his life. His standards, or his code of honor if you will, demand that he live a life of excellence. Because his code of honor involves much more than his martial skills, he realizes that there is much more to the warrior lifestyle than simply being experienced in the art of war or self-defense. He is engaged in a battle to conquer himself; the greatest victory is victory over one's self.

While it is true that martial arts training is a vital part of warriorship, it is not the sole component of a true warrior. There are many people who are trained fighters who are not true warriors. The world is full of killers, gang members, and people of low character who are well-versed in weapons and how to take a human life, but is this the singular requirement for being a warrior? Are these people true warriors or simply trained thugs? Anyone can learn to pull a trigger or destroy the human body. Does this knowledge make them a true warrior, or is there more to the warrior than the ability to fight?

Throughout the centuries, there have been both men of low character and men of exceptional character engaged in warfare. Although they both have been trained in the art of war, there is a significant difference in these two types of men. The true warrior is a man of character. There is more to him than his fighting skills. He is a man of wisdom and honor. His presence makes those around him safer. His code of honor requires that he protect those around him and only use his martial skills for defense and never for personal gain or selfish reasons.

The true warrior is not a programmed killing machine, although he has the ability and the knowledge to render lethal applications of his skills if his duty requires such extreme actions. Though he is capable of rendering devastating injury to others, he never desires to do so. He is a man of peace and benevolence. His training in the martial arts is strictly for defense. The warrior pursues knowledge in the art of war in order to keep himself and those around him safe, not for personal egotistical reasons.

Warriors have an independent spirit. The warrior is a man who thinks for himself and thinks rationally. I have had many people question me concerning some of the people who I quote in my writing. They question whether or not this man or that man is appropriate as a source of wisdom for the warrior because of his reputation or something that he did in his lifetime. My response is there are no perfect people. I believe that the warrior should use wisdom wherever he finds it. Wisdom can come from various and unpredictable sources. Whether it is a five year old child or a wino on a street corner, anyone can have a profound and insightful thought.

True wisdom is universal. Should we discard an enlightened thought simply because we are not impressed with the person who is used to communicate that thought to us? The true warrior knows that the purpose of wisdom is to improve his life and his character. Even if that wisdom comes from a five year old child or an old wino, he is not too proud to take what is said and meditate on it and apply it in his life. He thinks for himself and is not influenced by political correctness or the mind games that many people play.

Our currency all comes from government sanctioned mints and has value no matter whose pocket it happens to be at any given moment. In the same way, universal wisdom all comes from One Source and is useful in guiding the warrior on the warrior's path. It does not matter who the carrier of that wisdom may be, universal wisdom does not lose its value. The warrior knows this and uses his spirit as a guide to the truthfulness and validity of the thoughts of others. He uses what he finds useful and discards what strikes him as, "not quite right."

There are many sides to the warrior. True warriors not only develop their physical skills, but they also focus on perfecting their mental, emotional, and spiritual sides. They seek to find balance in their life and to bring every part of their life into alignment with that of the warrior ideals. The ideals of the warrior focus on principles which lead to personal fulfillment in every area of his life. Warriors seek to perfect each part of their life, not only their martial art skills.

The warrior lifestyle is one of taking one's life seriously, especially where honor, character, and integrity are concerned. It requires patience and self-discipline. It requires dedication and hard work. The true warrior is not willing to go through life as so many others do, passing each day as if they are on auto-pilot, in a semi-hypnotic state. He prefers to live life to the fullest, and to live by his own standards. He prefers to be totally awake and live in the present moment.

The warrior lifestyle is a lifestyle of excellence, discipline, service, honor, and character. It is a path that not many are willing to walk, but one which benefits all who dare to travel its steep terrain. Everyone has a decision to make concerning which life-path he will choose. Most choose the path of least resistance. Only a select few choose the path of the warrior, but those who do, find it worth the struggle. The warrior's path is a conduit of excellence. It is the path of the true human being – the warrior.

Live With Honor!

Bohdi Sanders, Ph.D.

The
Warrior
Lifestyle

1

The Way of a Warrior is based on humanity, love, and sincerity; the heart of martial valor is true bravery, wisdom, love, and friendship.
Morihei Ueshiba

When the ordinary person sees this quote, he thinks this is ridiculous, how can the "Way of the Warrior" be based on humanity or love? After all, the warrior trains in violent techniques. He learns how to destroy the body. He is proficient with weapons whose sole purpose is to be used against other human beings. How could anyone possibly make a statement such as the one above? This is what the average person on the street thinks when he thinks of the warrior, and it is a common misconception.

Those who truly understand the way of the warrior know what Morihei Ueshiba, the founder of Aikido, meant by this statement. The way of the warrior is based on the qualities of humanity, love, sincerity, bravery, wisdom, and friendship, among other outstanding qualities. No one in his right mind would risk his life for a stranger if he didn't have a heart full of love for humanity or a heart of valor and bravery. Many people mistakenly think of the warrior as a killing machine or a brute.

This kind of politically correct thinking is skewed. The true warrior is as far from being an uncivilized brute as east is from west. You will find that the majority of people simply do not understand the warrior lifestyle. They only focus on the fact that warriors train in dangerous skills that can be used to hurt other people. The fact that those skills are only used for the protection of the warrior, and those around the warrior, seems to elude them.

2

We must learn to reawaken
and keep ourselves awake.
Thoreau

No matter where you may find yourself, or in whatever kind of situation you may find yourself in, your first line of defense is being aware of your surroundings. Don't allow yourself to walk around in a mental fog. Be aware of what is going on around you. It doesn't matter if you are out at night in a seedy part of town, or if you are simply shopping for groceries in the middle of the day – be aware of your surroundings. The unexpected tragedy is never expected, this is why is it called an "unexpected" tragedy.

You never know when your path will cross paths with someone with less than honorable intentions. No one ever expects to find himself face to face with someone who is mentally unbalanced and wielding a gun in the grocery store or the department store, yet each year the media covers just this type of thing happening to unsuspecting citizens. These law abiding people are just going about their business when they are surprised by someone blasting away, randomly shooting whomever happens to be caught in the crosshairs.

This is why awareness is so important. You just never know when something like that will happen, but you have a much greater chance of surviving if you remain aware. This doesn't mean that you should walk around scared or in a constant state of fear, but only that you are aware of your surroundings when you are away from home. It is dangerous to walk around oblivious to your surroundings. Engage your mind. Don't be mentally lazy. Stay sharp.

3

Don't follow the advice of others; rather, learn to listen to the voice within yourself.
Dogen

This quote by Dogen, the famous 13th century Zen master, is a little misleading at first. When you first read it, it seems as though Dogen is telling us not to follow the advice of others. What he is actually telling us is not to *blindly* follow the advice of others, but rather to listen to the advice of others, while at the same time listening to your inner spirit. It is wise to listen to the advice and opinions of others, but always think for yourself. Don't act on the advice of others until you feel, deep in your spirit, that their advice is right.

This is what is meant by listening to the voice within. Always trust your internal voice, whether you call it your "small quiet voice," or your intuition, it will not lead you astray if you will learn to listen to what it is trying to tell you. How do you know what it is trying to tell you? You listen. You have to spend some quiet time alone, just you and your spirit. For many this is challenging. We are so used to the constant bombardment of external stimuli going on today that silence can actually feel awkward.

Listening is a skill that has to be developed just like your roundhouse kick or your side kick. Can you remember when you first began martial arts, how awkward some of the kicks and techniques were? Nothing that is completely new is comfortable at first. You have to practice new skills and techniques until you become comfortable with them and they become second nature. The same is true of listening to your intuition or your spirit. As Hui Neng taught, "Look within...The secret is in you."

4

Desire no revenge.
Masaaki Hatsumi

It is best to forgive a wrong done to you and move on. Benjamin Franklin said it this way, "Doing an injury puts you below your enemy; revenging one makes you but even with him; forgiving it sets you above him." Forgive and move on with your life. Don't let the person who has done you wrong continue to get the best of you by causing you unhappy, stress-filled thoughts on a daily basis. As the saying goes, living well is the best revenge.

Notice that I said you should forgive the person who has done you wrong. I did not say that you should forget about the matter. Don't allow your thoughts to dwell on it day in and day out, but don't completely forget about it either. You should remember what this person is capable of and the kind of man that he truly is deep inside. Don't be naïve enough to put yourself in a position where this person can wrong you a second time. That would be unwise.

The wise man, the warrior, will forgive and move on with his life, but at the same time keep this information filed away for future reference. Leopards don't change their spots, and men of low character rarely change their behavior. Hold no grudges, for resentments injure you much more than they injure your enemy, but at the same time don't trip over the same stump more than once. Deal with the incident, learn what you need to learn from what has happened, and continue down the path of the warrior. Seek no revenge, your enemy's karma will avenge you soon enough.

5

When you have to kill a man it costs nothing to be polite.
Winston Churchill

Being polite and respectful is not only a part of the martial arts, but is also a part of who the warrior is deep down inside. In any given dojo, you will see students bow when entering or exiting the training area. If you observe closely, you will notice that the majority of these "acts of respect" are done lackadaisically, with the student making a split second, half-hearted bow. One has to wonder if this is a real sign of respect or is it simply a mindless reflex.

Respect and honor comes from deep inside, it is not simply a physical action. If these students are not taking their time and thinking about why they are bowing before entering or exiting the dojo, why even bother? The warrior, as I have said before, takes things a little more seriously that the average person. Respect and politeness mean more to him than merely a learned routine that he mindlessly goes through at certain times. He gives thought to everything that he does.

This even applies to his enemies, as this quote by Churchill points out. You don't have to be rude or demeaning to your enemy, even if you are forced to get physical with him. Degrading someone else only speaks to your own character. It makes no difference whether they deserve to be treated with respect or not; that is the way you treat people because that is who you are as a warrior, not because they do or don't "deserve" it. To quote Clint Eastwood's character, William Money, "Deserve's got nothing to do with it."

6

In dangerous times
wise men say nothing.
Aesop

Aesop was a wise man. Great wisdom can be obtained from his fables and astute tales. This quote is no different; in fact it is one that the warrior should take to heart. In dangerous times wise men say nothing. When you find yourself in a bad situation or in circumstances beyond your control, silence can be the best course of action. Let others vent, yell, accuse, and lose their cool, while you silently listen and rationally consider what has happened, what is being said, and what to do next.

It is during times of stress that others will let their guard down and speak without thinking, often expressing thoughts which should be kept secret. Resist the urge to do this and just be silent. Let others make the mistake of losing their temper and saying things which could hurt them or for which they will later have to swallow their pride and apologize. The wise man will see this as a trap and as a chance to practice self-control by controlling his emotions.

This is not the same thing as being silent because of the fear of what could happen if you speak. Acting out of a sense of fear, and acting out of a sense of rational wisdom are two different things. Once again, your intentions play a major part in everything that you do. If your intent is to rationally control your emotions and act as a man of wisdom that is one thing, but if your intention is to be silent because you are afraid of doing what needs to be done, that is something entirely different. Make sure things are right on the inside.

7

Certain good qualities are like the senses: people entirely lacking in them can neither perceive nor comprehend them.
La Rochefoucauld

True warriors tend to associate with other warriors or with men of integrity and character. They find that they have to associate with men of honor because they are the only people with whom they can really talk. Other people just do not seem to comprehend what they are talking about, nor do they understand the warrior's values and principles most of the time. As La Rochefoucauld taught, many of the qualities of the warrior are foreign to most people.

They do not understand or comprehend how anyone could think like the warrior thinks. The ideals of the warrior are seen as outdated and useless to many in our society, and they have no problem stating just that. They do so without giving any regard to diplomacy or understanding. They totally lack these qualities and therefore cannot even perceive of anyone who would make these ideals an important part of his life.

For this reason, the warrior finds it more rewarding and less confrontational to associate with men who, like himself, are men of wisdom and honor. While it may be a tall order, he does not look down on those who lack the qualities which are so important to the warrior lifestyle, but rather feels empathy for those who live a less principled life. All the same, the warrior refuses to give up his ideals in order to fit in with those who choose the lower road. Each man must make his own path and live with his own decisions.

8

Rage and resentment
lead to rash action.
Sun Tzu

How many times have you heard someone say something to the effect of, "If I get mad, nothing can stop me?" Many people seem to have this attitude. The rush of adrenaline gives them the sense of unstoppable power and strength, but what they fail to realize is that their personal feelings of power and strength do not change their enemy's skills, strength or power. While it is true that a rush of adrenaline does bump you up a notch on the physical scale, it also comes at a price.

As your body is raging, your mind is disengaged. This means that you are no longer acting from a rational place. You have allowed your rage and anger to take control in place of your rational thought process. As Sun Tzu taught, this leads to rash actions which can many times cause you some major problems. The warrior should act from a place of rational consideration of each situation. He should act rather than react. This requires a calm mind.

While the warrior does need that rush of adrenaline, he has to learn to control it and use it. The warrior has to control his rage and anger, not let his rage and anger control him. This takes practice and self-control, and is developed through hours of realistic training and meditation. Don't give your power to anyone else or anything else. Maintain control at all times and remember that your mind is your best weapon, but only if you control your thoughts and think rationally.

9

Cowards die many times before their deaths, the valiant never taste of death but once.
Shakespeare

This famous quote from William Shakespeare is often used to justify unwise decisions. Don't use this wisdom to validate fighting when wisdom dictates that you should walk away. Walking away from a possible physical encounter does not indicate cowardice; it demonstrates wisdom. Many times it takes more courage to walk away from a fight, than it does to stay and slug it out.

Always consider your ultimate objective when you find yourself in this kind of situation. Don't confuse pride with courage. While it is true that it takes a certain amount of courage to fight, whether you are fighting out of necessity or fighting out of pride, it takes more courage to walk away when people are jeering at you, than it does to stand and fight. The warrior can walk away with his pride still intact because he knows in his heart that he is able to defend himself.

This is totally different from the man who walks away out of fear. The man, who walks away out of fear, although his action may look the same on the outside, is actually acting out of cowardice. His fear dictates his action, not his sense of duty or wisdom. It is true that it is probably a wise move for him to make, especially if he can't defend himself, but it is a totally different action than that of the warrior. Many times it is hard to interpret the actions of others as courageous or cowardly. The important thing is that you yourself know in your heart whether or not your actions are courageous.

10

Say but little, and say it well.
Irish Proverb

The great chief of the Nez Perce Indians, Chief Joseph, said that it takes very few words to speak the truth. This attitude concerning a man's speech is common throughout Native American culture. The Native Americans don't believe in rambling on and on about unimportant matters. They listen attentively to what others are saying, compose their thoughts, and then say what they need to say, and only what needs to be said. This approach to speaking ensures that your words have meaning.

People who talk a lot usually have very little wisdom to share. Of course there is always the exception to the rule, such as the elder who loves to share his knowledge with others and to teach the younger people through tales of the past. There is much wisdom to be gained by listening to these people, but the average person on the street who babbles on and on is usually sharing nothing of value and often merely seeks attention. His speech is void of wisdom, and much of what he says is false or skewed.

The warrior should strive to emulate the Native American traditions of speech. He should spend much more time listening and learning, than putting his two cents into the conversation. And when he does decide to enlighten those around him, he should do so with thought. He should say what needs to be said or what is profitable for those around him, and he should make every effort to say what he needs to say, with eloquence and tact. Develop the reputation of being a man that should be listened to when you speak.

11

No man ever becomes wise by chance.
Seneca

Wisdom and knowledge don't just appear out of the blue. Just as you must work hard to obtain your martial arts skills, you must study and contemplate to become wise. Even Confucius stated that he was not born knowing what he taught, but being fond of wisdom, he studied and worked to become a wise man. Anyone can become wise. It simply requires a sincere desire to study the wisdom of the past, and then reflect on that wisdom and make it your own.

Making wisdom your own requires much more than memorizing wise quotes or proverbs, and throwing them around like overused clichés. You must internalize what you study and be able to apply that wisdom to the changing circumstances of life. You must comprehend and internalize the underlying principles behind what the sages of the past codified for your benefit. This is the reason that the samurai studied "the ancient writings," they sought to gain insight and wisdom, not simply memorize the words of others.

The same applies to the modern day warrior. It is important that the true warrior gain wisdom. Without wisdom, it will be difficult for him to understand the true importance of living a life of character and honor. The fool and the common man do not understand the importance of such things because they lack this very wisdom to which I am referring. The true warrior seeks out wisdom, and along with his other qualities, he builds a reputation as a wise man.

12

There is much to be considered before the sword is drawn.
Baltasar Gracian

Fighting is serious business. Even when you win a physical conflict, there is a very real chance that you will not walk away from it unscarred. I have won many fights, but have ended up with the short end of the stick in the long run. Breaking a bone in your hand can take well over a year to heal. Sure, you may have won the fight, but the other guy's black eye and busted nose will be healed much sooner than your broken hand. This is only one of the many things that you must consider when it comes to fighting.

The bottom line is that you should never fight unless you have absolutely no other options. The warrior realizes this. He is not out to prove himself to others or to test his martial arts skills in the streets. Warriors know how fragile the human body is and how easily it can be damaged, especially by a skilled fighter. Fighting can cause more problems than you can imagine. It is not the carefree brawl which is depicted in so many movies and television shows.

Every fight carries with it the very real possibility of death, even if no one is consciously attempting to mortally injure the other person. Many people have died in fights which consisted of only one punch. People get hit, fall, and hit their head on something, and that's that. As Gracian states, there is definitely much to be considered before things get physical, and these things have to be considered ahead of time. You have to know what you are willing to fight for and how far you are willing to go *before* you find yourself in that spot.

13

If you are forced into a position in which you must either hurt or be hurt, be sure to make your move before someone else does.

Francesco Guicciardini

In the event of a physical threat or an attack, you cannot afford to wait to make your move. Many times it only takes one punch, one kick, or one slash with a knife to end an attack. If you wait until that punch, kick or slash has occurred, it is could be too late for you to come out of the encounter victorious. This is where the skill of personal awareness is crucial for the warrior. You have to be able to foresee the attack or threat before it actually materializes.

There should be no "first attack" in karate or in the warrior lifestyle for that matter, but the "first attack" is not necessarily physical. The first attack happens when you realize that someone means you harm. Once you know that someone means you harm, it is time for you to act, whatever that action may be. Your action does not necessarily have to be physical, but it definitely may be necessary to respond to the threat in a physical manner.

Your move will depend on the situation. Whether or not you make the first move will depend on your awareness and willingness to take action when action is required. Don't take the chance that your enemy will not follow through on his threat. Don't wait until it is too late to make your move. When you sense that first attack, respond with the appropriate response, whatever that may be. Different attacks require different responses, but all attacks or threats require some response, and it is always best to make your move first.

14

You must not show your weak points, either in the martial arts or in everyday life.
Taisen Deshimaru

It seems in today's society that people really enjoy talking about their illnesses or their injuries. People seem to derive some joy out of other people feeling sorry for them because of their hard life. They constantly want to tell you about their new problem, ache or pain. Sharing personal information seems to come naturally to them, even if other people are disinterested.

This is not a wise policy for the warrior to follow. By giving others information concerning your weak points, you are actually giving them information that can be used against you at some time down the road. Your enemies can store away information which may seem insignificant and meaningless, only to use it against you at some other time. For example, you may mention in casual conversation that you have a bum knee from an old football injury; this is something that someone can easily use against you in a fight.

Even though you may be speaking with someone whom you would never suspect to be your enemy, or who would never present any threat to you, people talk and you never know what will be repeated. Your friend has a friend, and that friend has a friend. It is best to keep you weak points private. Why take a chance that something you say will be used against you at some point? What does it benefit you to share your personal weaknesses with others? It is safer to keep your weaknesses, mistakes, and faults private. Don't talk just to hear yourself speak or to be the center of attention.

15

The wise man adapts himself to the circumstances.
Confucius

The warrior lives by a certain set of standards, a code of honor if you will. There are certain things that he will not do because those things go against his beliefs and the standards which he has set for himself. Many of his principles are not open to compromise; they are set in stone and he refuses to bend where they are concerned, but this does not mean that he is inflexible. Although the warrior is not willing to bend where his principles are concerned, he must be flexible in his strategy.

Warriors have to be able to adapt to the changing circumstances. The willow bends and adapts during the storm and is not broken, where the mighty oak does not bend and will break during the storm. The warrior must be able to change tactics as the situation changes. He will adapt his methods to that which the present circumstance requires. Not to do so would be foolish and costly.

This is not to say that the warrior should lower his standards or set aside his ethics as he sees fit. There is a difference in changing your strategy to fit the circumstances and in changing your ethics to suit the situation. This is where time spent meditating on your code of ethics and honor comes into play. You must be clear about what you believe and why you hold those beliefs. Change your methods to accomplish your goal; don't compromise your ethics to serve your methods. This may seem like a subtle distinction, but it is an important one, especially for the warrior.

16

Seek the friendship of the elderly.
Strabo

There is an ancient proverb which states that every time an elderly person dies, it is as if a library is burned to the ground. There is much to be learned from the elderly, and the wise man will take advantage of their wisdom and their friendship. Everyone should grow wiser as they grow older, and the older someone becomes, the more wisdom they should have amassed over the years. This aphorism is not set in stone; there are many elderly people who simply grow older, not wiser, but overall it is true.

Not only can you benefit from the wisdom gained from their many years of observing how men act and react, but it is the duty of the superior man to respect and help the elderly, both in their family and in their community. The warrior realizes this. He knows that part of the warrior lifestyle in rooted in service to others, especially the elderly and those who need his help. Not all elderly people have family members to take care of them or to help them with their needs. The warrior should step up and provide assistance when he can.

When you see a need that an elderly person has, whether it is yard work or help bringing in their groceries, offer your assistance. Service does not simply mean stepping in and protecting someone who is being mugged or harassed. It also means helping those in your community who need your help. It may even be as simple as taking a little time to sit and listen to an elderly friend reminisce about old times over a cup of tea. You never know when very little will mean a great deal to someone in need.

17

The more quickly brought to anger, the more quickly brought to death.
Chinese Maxim

The sages have always taught the dangers of allowing your anger to control your actions. They have taught throughout the ages, that you must control your anger. You must think rationally, not emotionally. Anger does not allow for rational thought. When your emotions are raging and your adrenaline is pumping, you do not think rationally. You have to control your anger in order to think properly.

This principle has been proven throughout the ages. It has always been a successful tactic in battle, whether between armies or between individuals, to anger your opponent in order to cause him to make mental mistakes, mistakes that could cost him his life. Taunting, abrasive language, rude actions, etc. are all actions which your enemy will use against you in order to rile you and cause you to act rashly. Once you have allowed your anger to control your actions, he has accomplished his goal.

His goal is to upset you and draw you into his trap by disabling your ability to think rationally. As the maxim above states, the sooner this happens, the sooner you are finished. This is a sucker's game. See it for what it really is, and don't get suckered into that trap. Turn the tables on him. It is very frustrating for your enemy, who is trying his best to anger you, when you don't get angry. So much so that his tactic can actually backfire, and many times, he is the one who gets angry and loses control. See this game for the ruse that it is. Be smart.

18

Honor is not black and white.
Forrest E. Morgan

Many people have a warped sense of honor. Some use their sense of honor to justify stupid decisions. For example, someone may think that he is "too honorable" to fight dirty. As I have said before, this is simply an unintelligent decision, but there are many people who view honor in terms of black or white. It is admirable that they at least have a sense of honor, even though their concept of honor is misguided and could cause them difficulty in certain situations.

Many people fail to even consider the significance of honor. To them, honor is a meaningless concept that went out of fashion with the knights of old. They couldn't care less about being honorable or whether their actions are right or wrong. They will tell you point blank that honor is a ridiculous concept. These are people with questionable ethics and not people with whom the warrior wants to associate. Many times it is easy to tell if someone is totally lacking in honor. Dishonor is more easily discerned than honor.

Honor is not a black and white set of rules which the warrior must abide by during his life. There is not one code of honor that is set in stone. As Samuel Coleridge wrote, "Our own heart, and not other men's opinion, form our true honor." The warrior lives by a code of honor, but honor is much more complicated than many make it out to be. Honor is bound by intention, and no man is privy to another man's intention. Therefore, it is only the warrior himself who truly knows whether or not he is an honorable man.

19

The wise focus their attention inside.
Lao Tzu

What does it mean to focus your attention inside? Is Lao Tzu talking about introspection or is he referring to meditation? To the warrior, it doesn't really matter which of these Lao Tzu is referring to because both are important to the warrior lifestyle. Not only does the warrior need to make meditation a part of his daily routine, but he should also spend time in self-reflection.

Self-knowledge is a vital part of being a warrior. You have to know yourself inside and out. Know your weaknesses and your strengths. Be aware of what your "hot buttons" are so that you can recognize when someone is attempting to push them and throw you off your game. You should know the limits of your abilities and judge yourself honestly. Look at yourself as you are, not as you wish you were, at least where your talents are concerned.

Sun Tzu taught that you must know yourself in order to be victorious against your enemy, "If you know the enemy and know yourself, you need not fear the result of a hundred battles. If you know yourself but not the enemy, for every victory gained you will also suffer a defeat. If you know neither the enemy nor yourself, you will succumb in every battle." I cannot emphasize strongly enough the importance of thoroughly knowing yourself. Focus your attention inside, not just during your meditation time, but also during quiet times when you can really reflect on who you truly are and where your abilities lie.

20

The world is a dangerous place, not because of those who do evil, but because of those who look on and do nothing.
Albert Einstein

I think that this statement by Albert Einstein would be more accurate if he had stated that the world is a dangerous place *not only* because of those who do evil, *but also* because of those who look on and do nothing. There are some very dangerous, evil people in this world. That is just the way it is, and if anyone disputes that, they are living in a fantasy world. Some people are just plain bad and will kill you at the drop of a hat, and then order a Big Mac as if nothing had happened.

As bad as that sounds (and it is pretty bad), Einstein considered those people less of a problem than the people who look on and do nothing. Can you see his point? If everyone took an active role in bringing the evil people to justice, swift and sure justice, the evil doers would become less and less prevalent. Even though there are a lot of evil men in this world, there are many, many more people who allow them to exist because of their apathy or fear. Those who allow evil, condone evil.

This world is a dangerous place both because of evil men and because of the apathy of others. This is why it is so important that the warrior be prepared to recognize and confront evil. If the warrior is not willing to stand up and do something about the evil in this world, who will? Can you rid this world of evil by protecting those around you? No. Can you make those around you safer, simply because you are there with them? Absolutely!

21

There is no such thing as a fair fight.
Bohdi Sanders

The idea of fighting dirty is viewed almost as a form of profanity in the majority of martial arts dojos today. Many instructors would shutter if one of their students suggested using a brick during a fight, or throwing sand in his enemy's eyes during a physical confrontation. After all, this is just not honorable, right? The superior man, the warrior, is not supposed to "fight dirty." Isn't he is supposed to live by the highest standards at all times?

Many people are confused on this point. Allow me to make it completely clear. When you are in a serious fight to protect yourself or others, there is no such thing as fighting dirty; there is only victory or defeat. You should have no compunction about using any and all tactics to defeat your attacker and come out victorious. This includes everything from using bricks and throwing sand, to using broken glass and gouging the eyes.

Yes these are very serious actions to take, but what many people don't seem to understand is that an attack on the street is a very serious situation. Serious situations call for a serious response. This has nothing to do with the warrior's honor. Your honor is still intact if you have done everything in your power to prevent this situation from happening in the first place. Don't let your false perception of honor cost you when dealing with others, especially in a physical confrontation.

22

Don't protect people who don't deserve it. Your job is to protect the good. Observe one's true character.
Masaaki Hatsumi

I have stated many times that it is the warrior's duty to protect others. Serving and protecting others who do not have the ability or know-how to protect themselves is part of the warrior lifestyle, but does this mean that you are duty bound to protect everyone, all the time? According to Masaaki Hatsumi, the Ninjutsu grandmaster and founder of the Bujinkan Organization, the warrior should only protect those who deserve it.

This brings us to the question of who deserves your protection and who does not deserve your protection. How do you know? Masaaki Hatsumi goes on to explain that it is your job, as a warrior, to protect the good. Again, how do you know who is good and who is not? You observe people's true character. Yes, this may involve personal judgments concerning other people, but a wise warrior will make some judgments before placing his life on the line to help someone.

Would you consider it your duty to help a pimp who is being pounded on the street by some drug dealer for a personal disagreement between these two dishonorable men? I wouldn't. But this situation would be different if the drug dealer was pounding some innocent school boy. There is a big difference, and it requires your discernment to make the call. Serve and protect, but use good judgment. Protect the good and let the wicked live with the consequences of their actions.

23

To be prepared beforehand for any contingency is the greatest of virtues.
Sun Tzu

The Boy Scouts have it right – "Be Prepared." The warrior should focus his attention on being as prepared as possible for whatever may come his way. Of course it is basically impossible to be prepared for every possible thing that could happen, but you can train your mind to remain calm and to think rationally regardless of the situation at hand. Learning to keep a calm, rational mind in the midst of turmoil is one way of being prepared for the unexpected.

Meditation is one way to train your mind to remain calm and tranquil. The more that you meditate, the more you will find that your mind is able to stay calm under pressure. Breathing techniques also help you to maintain your balance during times of stress. Those who work under high pressure situations find that autogenic breathing techniques enable them to maintain their composure when their back is against the wall.

Of course, it goes without saying that your martial arts training prepares you to meet physical confrontations with strength and confidence. You must continue to maintain you skills to be prepared for the unexpected trouble that you may encounter on the street. This doesn't apply only to your martial arts techniques, but to your meditation and your breathing techniques also. If you do not practice all of these things, they will not be available to you when you find that you need them. This is part of what it means to be prepared.

24

In war there is
no substitute for victory.
Douglas MacArthur

This sentiment from Douglas MacArthur seems to have been forgotten in our modern culture. People seem to want to candy-coat things and discuss how you should fight fair or not lower yourself to the level of your enemy. This touchy-feely attitude sounds wonderful. It certainly makes you appear socially acceptable, but it doesn't hold water in the real world for one important reason – it is unrealistic.

When you are engaged with an enemy in a life-or-death situation, and you are "playing" by a set of rules which your enemy neither plays by nor respects, you have just handicapped yourself and your chances for victory. You are handicapped even more if you publicize the fact that you will "play" by those rules no matter what. No matter what weapon is pulled or how dire the situation, "we will not scratch, kick, bite, or hit below the belt."

That is ridiculous! There is no substitute for victory. In a serious physical confrontation, you must use whatever you can to ensure that you are not only victorious, but that you also come out of the encounter with as few injuries as possible. There is no such thing as fighting fair in a life-or-death confrontation. That is only a myth. There are no rules except to win the battle and walk away with your life. I can assure you that your enemy will not be fighting fair; he will use anything and everything that he can to accomplish his goal.

25

True Budo has an overwhelming emphasis on the development of moral character.
Glenn Morris

Budo is the Japanese term for martial arts, and the martial arts should indeed have an overwhelming emphasis on developing one's moral character. The key word in this quote is "true." "True" budo has an emphasis on the development of moral character. But how many martial arts schools today really focus on the development of moral character? Can these schools which do not focus on the moral character of the student really be called true martial arts schools or are they simply teaching fighting techniques?

This is not only a distinction between the true martial arts schools and the schools which are only there to make money, but it is also the distinction between the true warrior and the man who is only trained to fight. The true warrior will not only be focused on his martial skills, but he will also be dedicated to the perfection of his character. Without this important ingredient, there is no warrior, only someone trained to be dangerous, just another possible menace to society.

Gichin Funakoshi stated that the ultimate goal of karate lies neither in victory or defeat, but rather in the perfection of the character of its participants. This is true for the path of the warrior. The ultimate objective for the warrior is the perfection of his character, everything else is simply tools which he uses to achieve his objective. This is the main trait that separates the true warrior from his counterparts. He is just as capable of rendering destruction as they are, but he is coming from a place of true honor and character, and therefore can be relied on to be a just man – a true warrior.

26

Adversity is a mirror
that reveals one's true self.
Chinese Proverb

You never really know what you can do until you have had your limits tested through extreme adversity. No matter how much training you have had or how much time you have spent pondering certain situations, it is all speculation until you go through the experience of true hardship or danger. It is during these times that your true self comes to the surface and reveals who you really are. You can no longer bluff your way through, if indeed that is what you have been doing (hopefully it is not what you have been doing).

The bully can talk the talk, but often when someone stands up to him, we find that it has all been a bluff. He is not the tough guy that he portrayed himself to be. This never comes to light until someone calls his bluff and reveals his true nature. It is through adversity that we actually know who someone really is deep inside. During times of hardship people tend to give up their concern over their image and the true self appears.

Most people have a carefully protected façade built around them. This is the image that they present to the public, and many times it is quite different from who they truly are as a person. The warrior's true self and the everyday image that he portrays should be one and the same. He has no need to hide his true self because he lives his life as a man of honor and is prepared for the hardships and dangers which he may face during his lifetime. He is a man of sincerity. When he looks into the mirror of adversity, he simply sees the same image that he sees every day – the warrior.

27

All men make mistakes, but a good man yields when he knows his course is wrong, and repairs the evil.
Sophocles

The warrior is many things. He is a man of honor, integrity and character. He is a man of courage and a hero if need be. He is a superior man in the sense of his lifestyle and character. But there is one thing that he is not – a perfect man. All men make mistakes, including the warrior. All of his decisions will not be correct, even though he will try his best to make them so. There will be times when he slips and makes mistakes that he will regret; this is simply part of being human.

What makes the true warrior different in this regard is the fact that when he does make mistakes and he knows he is on the wrong path, he is man enough to make the necessary changes to his course. He owns up to his mistakes, learns from them, meditates on what changes he needs to make, and then makes those changes. If his mistake has hurt someone or caused damage in any way, he does his best to make amends and right any wrongs which may have been caused by his mistake.

Personal responsibility is the hallmark of the true warrior. He alone knows that his true intentions were honorable, but still he knows that he is responsible for the results of his actions nonetheless. Knowing that his intentions were honorable, he is not ashamed to take this responsibility. He makes his own decisions and then deals with the results of those decisions as they present themselves. This is the way of the superior man – the way of the warrior.

28

A wise man, in great or small matters, must act with due consideration.
Sakya Pandit

To the man of excellence, everything matters, even the small stuff. The warrior is a man of excellence and will take pains to do everything that he does to the best of his ability. It doesn't matter whether he is dealing with a life-or-death situation or making a new flower bed for his wife in his backyard, he will give his full attention to the task at hand. Small mistakes can turn into big headaches. The warrior knows this and thus acts with due consideration in every area of his life.

Think back throughout your life and consider how many times you have made quick, thoughtless decisions which have come back to haunt you at a later date. Wouldn't it have been much better to have taken the time to stop and think before you made those decisions? Many times we allow ourselves to hurry and make decisions without giving them much thought or consideration concerning the possible consequences, and many times this ends up saving us no time at all, but rather costing us time down the line.

Stop and think before you act. It doesn't matter if you are doing something that you consider important or whether you are doing something trivial – THINK. Always stay conscious of your actions and be in the moment. Not only is this smart, but it is also good practice for keeping your mind sharp and aware. Don't let yourself get into the habit of mindlessly going through the motions of life without thinking. Stay focused, whether dealing with small matters or a life-threatening situation. Always think before you act.

29

Brave hearts do not back down.
Euripides

Euripides tells us that brave hearts do not back down. However, this doesn't mean that brave hearts are stubborn or foolhardy. Brave hearts do not back down concerning their principles and important matters regarding their ideals. They show courage in the face of danger and hardship, but at the same time they think rationally and act with acute focus toward accomplishing their objective. They do not let their pride or their emotions control their decisions.

While it is true that brave hearts do not back down, this does not mean that there is never a time for the warrior to retreat and regroup. Your strategy must be flexible. Don't be hard-headed in your approach. As the circumstances of the moment change, so must your tactics and strategies change. When you see that the situation is not going your way and that your efforts need to be modified in order to achieve your goals, be willing to rethink your position and make the needed adjustments.

I have heard many men make comments such as, "They may kill me, but I will never back down." Well, that may be true, but does that accomplish your objective? Not unless your objective is to put up a good fight and be killed. Always focus on accomplishing your objectives, not on saving your pride. When thoughts such as the one above enter your mind, you know that you are now allowing pride and emotions to control your thinking instead of rational thought. Retreating and regrouping is not the same as backing down; do not confuse the two.

30

The brave and generous have the best lives. They're seldom sorry.
The Havamal

This may seem like strange wisdom coming from a culture which is known more for it vicious raids and fighting skills, than for its wisdom, but it holds true nonetheless. *The Havamal*, the ancient book of wisdom from the Viking culture, teaches that two kinds of people have the best lives – the brave and the generous. Though the Vikings were known for their bravery, they weren't really known for their generosity. The brave and the generous do seem to live good lives.

Courage is required to live life your way, to go against the tide and stand for your own principles. Without courage, all of the other virtues may be rendered useless. After all, what good are virtues if you do not have the intestinal fortitude to put them into action? Those without courage are easily swayed to put their virtue and honor on the shelf when they are inconvenient or when peer pressure is pushing hard against them. Virtue is impotent without courage.

Generosity is another trait that leads to a satisfying life. It is part of the warrior's duty to be generous to others. All of the sages throughout the ages have taught that it is better to give than to receive. There is something about being generous and helping others which does your own heart good, not to mention the fact that when you are kind to others your kindness will ultimately return to you. Help others whenever you can. Try to make everyone's life that you come into contact with a little better. Be brave and generous.

31

Proverbs are short sentences drawn from long experience.
Cervantes

If you have done much study in the field of wisdom literature, you will notice that many of the same proverbs, although they may be worded a bit different, are found in many different cultures throughout the world. The words may be different, but the underlying meaning is consistent from culture to culture. The reason behind this phenomenon is that true wisdom is universal. Some things are just common to the human race, no matter what language is spoken or what cultural norms are followed.

There are traits that are part of human nature and these traits happen to be universal enough that we find the same teachings throughout the world. How could this be and how do we know that proverbs are actually wise sayings that we can follow and count on to be true? Well, as Cervantes stated, proverbs are drawn from much experience. You could think of proverbs as common sense, although common sense is so rare that proverbs seem like deep wisdom to most people, and in fact most are full of insight and wisdom.

The wise man will learn from the mistakes and experiences of others instead of learning everything the hard way – through his own mistakes. This is where you can benefit from proverbs, as well as other wisdom writings. Learn from the experience of others. Benefit from what has been learned through ages of observing human behavior and character traits. Spend time studying wisdom literature and remember that true wisdom is universal. It is just as relevant today as it was the day it was written. Learn from the sages.

32

He who lives without discipline dies without honor.
Icelandic Proverb

It requires discipline to live a life of honor. It is not the easiest path, which is why there are so few people who choose to walk the path of honor. The man of honor makes certain sacrifices in order to live a life of honor, although to him, these sacrifices are more than worth it and are rarely seen as sacrifices at all. He doesn't understand how others live their lives paying little or no attention to the demands of honor. To him, it is unthinkable to live any other way.

Even so, this doesn't mean that a life of honor comes without hard work and intentionally cultivating it on a daily basis. Honor, like most other virtues, does not come automatically, but rather it has to be purposely developed over time. It takes discipline, discipline which most do not care to employ in their lives, and thus never really develop the character trait of true honor. To the common man, it is simply easier to live with "situational honor" where he is honorable most of the time, but his honor is not set in stone.

The warrior, on the other hand, looks at honor a bit differently. To the warrior, honor is not simply nice to have when it is convenient; it is an integral part of his life. Moreover, he takes pains to develop his code of honor and knows exactly what being honorable entails. He knows the truth behind the proverb above. He knows that if you live without discipline, you will have no choice but to die without honor because without discipline, there can be no honor.

33

In critical times, one must be devoted utterly to the cause of justice.
Gichin Funakoshi

Why did Master Funakoshi state that you must be completely devoted to the cause of justice in critical times? What makes critical times any more special than everyday times? The answer is simple. When your back is against the wall, and it is decision time, if you are not utterly devoted to justice, then you will falter and you will compromise your standards, your honor, and your character. It is these critical times which show your true character to the world.

The man who is not one-hundred percent devoted to justice, honor and integrity, will compromise himself when times get tough. Oh, he will justify his decision by saying things such as, "I had no choice. My neck was on the line." There are hundreds of ways to justify compromising your honor, but none of those justifications will placate the soul of the warrior who has just made concessions where his honor is concerned. Honor cannot be saved by excuses and justifying wrong actions.

You have to make a firm decision concerning your code of honor or code of ethics, and you must be totally devoted to being a man of honor, especially during critical times. Warriors take justice seriously, just as they take their honor seriously. There is no room for situational or counterfeit honor among those who profess to be true warriors. You are either a man of honor, or you are not. There is no middle ground. Be utterly devoted to your code of honor and to the cause of justice. Be a true warrior.

34

You can also commit injustice
by doing nothing.
Marcus Aurelius

There are many ways in which a man can be unjust. The warrior's actions must be just. Justice is at the center of the warrior's thoughts. He strives to do what is right and just at all times. It is his aim to make all of his actions right according to the standards which he lives. He would never consider acting in such a way as to purposely commit an injustice on another human being. But he must consider that refusing to act is an action in itself.

This is a foreign concept to many people. Doing nothing is actually doing something. You are deciding that your action during a certain time period is to sit still, in essence, to not act, and you are just as responsible for the results of this action as you are for any of your other actions. For example, if you see someone get hit by a car and you are in a position to help, but you choose to do nothing, you are responsible for the consequences of that choice. You may not be held responsible by our legal system, but the warrior lives by a higher law than the law of the land.

This is what Marcus Aurelius is saying when he says, "You can also commit injustice by doing nothing." In the example above, you have committed an injustice to the person who was hit by the car. You did not run over that person. You did not take his wallet while he was lying in the street unconscious, but you did commit an injustice nonetheless, by doing nothing and refusing to help someone in need when you could have taken action. The Warrior code demands that you help, protect and serve those who are deserving.

35

Moderation in temper is always a virtue; but moderation in principle is always a vice.
Thomas Paine

There is a time and a place for everything, well almost everything. As Thomas Paine stated, there is really not a time or a place to compromise on your principles. Your principles are your underlying codes that you live by. They are your ethical standards. They define you. It is the warrior's principles which make him what he is. Without them, he would be no different than any other man, with the possible exception that he is a trained fighter.

It is wise to use moderation in most things, but not in your underlying principles. Moderation in your principles is nothing more than compromising your code of honor, which as Paine put it, is always a vice. The warrior cannot compromise his principles without compromising who he is as a person. It is his principles which comprise his character, and his character which makes him a true warrior.

Courage is one of the traits of the warrior, and it is one of the most important traits, for without courage it is impossible to live by your principles at all times. It takes a lot of courage to stand up for your beliefs, especially when you are in the minority. Don't compromise on your principles. Have the courage to do what you know is right, even if everyone else is against you. Stand for what you believe in and let others be the ones who have to live with their lack of courage and loss of honor.

36

Prepare your minds for action;
be self-controlled.
The Apostle Paul

Every single martial artist that I have ever met seems to understand the importance of preparing his or her body for action. They may not do so for a multitude of reasons, but they do know the importance of keeping their bodies in shape, especially if they plan on using their martial arts for actual self-defense. This is a basic part of martial arts, but it seems that very few of these same martial artists realize the importance of preparing their minds for action. After all, your mind doesn't have to be "in shape" in order for you to defend yourself, right? Wrong!

It is just as important to prepare your mind for action as it is to prepare your body for action. All the martial arts training in the world will do you no good if your mind freezes or panics during the crucial moment of action. You have to train your mind to stay calm, focused, and rational at all times. You have to prepare your mind to deal with fear and to be able to act rationally, even when emotions such as fear, anger, and rage try to take control.

Mental training is as important as physical training for the warrior. Forms of mental training include meditation, realistic training scenarios, and visualization practice. The warrior must know how to act without having to slow down and do battle with his emotions, especially in the heat of the moment. A moment's delay can cost you dearly during a physical confrontation. Prepare your mind and your body for action.

37

We should know what our convictions are, and stand for them...
Carl Jung

It is pretty hard to live by your convictions when you don't know what they are, much less have total faith that your convictions are right. Living by your convictions means that you live according to your beliefs. Your convictions are your firmly held beliefs about certain things in your life or in the world. These beliefs are part of what makes you who you are as a warrior, and you should be completely clear concerning your deeply held convictions.

You only truly understand your convictions completely when you take the time to meditate on your beliefs. You have to spend quiet time alone with your thoughts in order to really identify with your personal beliefs or convictions. Most people do not take the time to do this, and therefore, do not really know what they believe or what their convictions are and why they should stand for them. For this reason, the majority of people today either don't have strong convictions, or their convictions are molded by others.

If your convictions are dictated to you by other people, they aren't really your convictions. You have simply adopted someone else's beliefs as your own, and unless you take those beliefs and meditate on them, you will never truly make them personal. This is why so many people are willing to compromise their principles. They say that they believe certain things, but they don't know why they believe them. Therefore, they aren't actually personal convictions, but rather borrowed beliefs which they can take or leave.

38

Individuals create karma;
karma does not create individuals.
Bodhidharma

Your actions create your karma, not the other way around. Karma is simply the law of cause and effect. Everything that you do, everything that you say, and everything that you think, carries with it some effect. There is a specific consequence connected to everything that the warrior does, no matter how small or how inconsequential. Nothing is immune to the law of karma, not even your thoughts.

Many people will argue this point and state that they can think whatever they please and there is no consequence connected to their thoughts, but this is not quite right. Your thoughts are strong forces. They have the power to change your emotions, the chemical make-up of your body, and ultimately they control your actions. This is just one example of how something as seemingly trivial as a thought, can have far reaching consequences that we never really consider.

Karma is like that in every part of our lives. Every single thing that happens in your life could be traced back to a cause if we had the ability or insight to do this exercise. Nothing happens without some cause behind it. People create karma. We are in control, not karma. If you don't like the things that are happening in your life, then change your actions, change your speech, change your thoughts, and you will change your future. You make the decisions, and ultimately, you have to live with the consequences of those decisions. If you needed yet another reason to live a life of honor and integrity – now you have it.

39

Let the wise man take refuge in his silence.

Baltasar Gracian

The babbling buffoon – we have all seen him. He is not a rare creature. In fact, you can witness the behavior of this man almost anywhere that you go, whether it be the local restaurant or the grocery store, you are sure to find this amazing individual. He is easy to recognize, just use your ears and listen; his speech always gives him away. You will recognize him by his relentless jabbering about nothing and everything at the same time, and his willingness to repeatedly put his foot in his mouth.

Listening to this foolish man for long is tiresome and fairly fruitless. There is little wisdom that flows from his lips, yet he never tires of sharing what little information he has to impart. If he has read it, heard it, sensed it, or just plain imagined it, don't worry, he will freely communicate it to you at lightning speed, and he will embellish it free of charge. He wouldn't want you not to be entertained! He craves your attention, although there is little in what he has to say that is worthy of your consideration.

Throughout the ages the sages have warned the wise man to not be like the man who talks incessantly without giving any thought or regard to what he is saying. Don't be like this poor creature who hangs himself over and over with the words from his own lips. Be like the wise man and take refuge in silence. It is not necessary to communicate everything that you know or everything that you think. In fact, it is unwise to do so. One of the traits of the true warrior is his ability to control his tongue. Think before you speak.

40

The truth simply is that's all. It doesn't need reasons; it doesn't have to be right; it's just the truth. Period.
Carl Frederick

The truth is the truth, period. It doesn't matter if it is not pretty. It doesn't matter if it is not what you want to hear. It doesn't matter if it goes against everything that you think that you know. None of these things have any impact on the truth. The truth simply is the truth. As Carl Frederick stated, it doesn't need any reasons, it doesn't need any explanations, it doesn't have to be right, and it doesn't have to be pleasing. It just is. It is as simple as that.

Sounds pretty straightforward doesn't it? Well, if it is so straightforward, why it is so hard to find out what the truth actually is? The answer lies in the manipulation of those willing to be manipulated. Most people take things at face value. When they are told that something is a certain way, they are willing to believe it. They believe the best in people instead of looking at someone's underlying motives. While this may be a peaceful, relaxing way to go through life, it also allows others to manipulate the truth.

The warrior has to be smart enough to look beyond the veil of deceit which precedes and cloaks many truths. Realize that not everyone lives by the same principles that you live by, and that those who don't live by the principles of honor, have very little problem stretching the truth to suit their personal objectives. Be smart enough to see through the lies. Things are as they are, whether you know the truth or not. Seek the truth, even if you don't like what you find. There is never any advantage in deceiving yourself, or in being deceived.

41

Things are not always what they seem; the first appearance deceives many; the intelligence of a few perceives what has been carefully hidden.
Phaedrus

Don't take things at face value. Always take the time to hear both sides of the story before you make up your mind about something, especially something important. Even after you have heard both sides of the story, it is prudent to always remember that each of those "sides" are merely someone's recollection of what happened. Most people, even when they are trying to be honest, will recall things through their own perception, which may or may not be accurate.

Almost everyone tends to embellish or put their own personal spin on things, especially when they are trying to persuade others to see their point of view. Things are not always exactly as they have been presented to you. It is wise to not only hear both sides, but to also do a little investigating on your own, particularly when the matter at hand is very important. Don't rely on hearsay. Remember that a lot of people today see nothing wrong with lying to you if they feel it will personally help their cause.

Be wise enough to understand that things are often not what they seem. Don't be deceived. Be cautious concerning what you believe and who your trust. Always bear in mind that not everyone lives by the principles that the warrior lives by, principles of honesty and integrity. It is foolish to put your trust in those who do not hold honor and integrity in high regard. Those who do are simply offering themselves up to as easy prey. Don't depend on the honesty of others; depend on your ability to discern the truth.

42

A warrior faces a double challenge: confronting the evil of others while resisting the darkness within. If he gives in to the latter, he becomes nothing more than a thug.
Wim Demeere

I have used Dave Grossman's analogy of the warrior as a sheepdog before, but it is appropriate to use again, especially where this quote by Wim Demeere is concerned. The sheepdog would enjoy a good, roasted leg of lamb just as much as the wolf. He is certainly not opposed to eating meat. He has canine teeth specifically meant for the ripping and chewing of meat. The difference between him and the wolf is that he is not willing to use his powerful jaws to kill that innocent lamb simply to satisfy his selfish desires.

The wolf does not care about the innocent lamb. He only cares about his own selfish appetite and cannot resist taking what he wants. This can be likened to the human predator. It is the duty of the sheepdog (the warrior) to protect the sheep (the average citizen) from the wolves (the predators). Sure the sheepdog has just as much ability to take advantage of the sheep's peaceful nature as the wolf does, but he has made a decision to protect the sheep instead of prey on them, while at the same time he confronts the wolf.

It is the warrior's duty to protect people and to use his martial arts for defense and not as a tool for intimidation or for selfish gains. Even while resisting the evil doers he may encounter, he must resist the urge to completely destroy them unless he has no other choice. By doing so, he is resisting the darkness within himself and choosing a higher, nobler path. If he doesn't control his inner urge to use his martial arts freely when he is angered he becomes no different than the thug.

43

Keep over your actions an absolute empire.
Thomas a'Kempis

You are the only person in the world who controls your actions. This is a fact. You make the decision concerning everything that you do. Now, you may want to argue this fact with statements such as, "That is not true. My boss tells me what to do," but this argument does not hold water. Your boss may tell you what to do, but ultimately it is you who makes the final decision concerning whether or not you do this or that. You, and nobody else, are in charge of your actions.

This is very important to realize because as the only person in the world who is capable of deciding what you will and what you will not do, you are also the only person in the world who is responsible for those actions. With power comes responsibility. You have the power to decide what you will and will not do, and therefore you have to take the responsibility for whatever action you decide to carry out. It is as simple as that – your choice, your responsibility.

This is the reason that Thomas a'Kempis stated that you should keep an absolute empire where your actions are concerned. You must not allow your emotions or fears to influence your actions. Every action should be considered from a rational point of view. You should think before you act, not try to figure out how to do damage control after the fact. The warrior realizes this and consequently he takes his actions more seriously than the average person on the street. Think self-control.

44

The Universal Way is not just a matter of speaking wisdom, but one of continual practice.
Lao Tzu

It does no good to study wisdom or to sit around and talk about wisdom with your peers, if you do not practice wisdom. The same goes for honor, integrity, character, and all the other traits that are a part of the warrior lifestyle. As Lao Tzu taught, the way is not simply a matter of speaking about things, but one of continual practice. If the traits of the warrior lifestyle are not put into action in the life of the warrior, they are worthless. Skills unused are of no benefit.

The warrior lifestyle in not about imagination or fantasy; it is about developing your life to the highest possible point. The warrior is a man of excellence in everything he does. He is a doer, not a talker. The man who simply talks a good talk, but never follows through on what he professes, is not a warrior, but rather a want-to-be warrior. He may know the language of the warrior, but he has not committed to live the warrior lifestyle.

On the other hand, the warrior takes his chosen path too seriously to merely talk about things such as honor and integrity, without making them a vital part of his everyday life. This is not a game to the true warrior; this is who he is. He is a man of wisdom, integrity and honor. He is sincere in his quest for the elusive perfection of character. He not only talks the talk, but he also walks the walk. Be a doer, not a talker. Take the path of the warrior seriously and it will reward you greatly.

45

Shun any action that will diminish honor.
Tiruvalluvar

When you have a decision to make and you are back forth about what to do, the first thing that you must look at in order to make the right choice is whether or not the action is honorable. If the action in question is dishonorable or will in any way go against your code of honor, don't even consider it. It is as simple as that. Any action that will diminish your honor is not the right path for you to take, even if it seems that it might be, for whatever reason.

If your honor is compromised, you have chosen the wrong action. In order for your code of honor to be meaningful, it must be unbending. Don't compromise where your principles are involved. Don't be willing to put your honor on the shelf for a period of time in order to perform an action that you know full well goes against your code of honor. Doing this reveals that your commitment to honor is weak and that you don't really take it that seriously, but it is simply a convenience rather than an integral part of your life.

Your honor must be more important to you than the many other things that tempt you to act in ways which might cause you to violate your code. Men of true honor will place their honor above personal gain or profit. There will be things which they will refuse to do, even if they find them enjoyable or profitable, simply because their honor forbids them to be done. The warrior puts his code of honor first in his life, and by doing so he finds that everything else falls into place. Live with honor.

46

The success of very important matters often depends on doing or not doing something that seems trivial.
Francesco Guicciardini

To the warrior, the trivial things are just as important as the crucial things. He strives to do everything that he does to the highest level. He is a man who seeks excellence, even in the smallest acts, which is a good thing when you consider this quote by Francesco Guicciardini. Many times it is the small things, which have been neglected, that lead to the failure of your goals or objectives.

Everything matters. Don't take the seemingly inconsequential things for granted because you believe that they don't matter. Strive to be complete. If something is worth doing, it is worth doing well. This includes the small things as well as the "important" things. By taking the time to ensure that everything is taken care of, every "t" is crossed and every "i" is dotted, you know that you have done the best that you can do.

Doing your very best in every undertaking gives you peace of mind. After all, if you have done the best that you can do, and have left nothing to chance, your conscience is free. You know that you have done all that you can do. What else is there? Also, by approaching everything in your life with this attitude, you will find that you will have fewer hassles and more success. When the foundation is solid, the rest will fall into place. Take nothing for granted; that which seems trivial may be the cornerstone to your success.

47

It is best to leave alone the
things that do not concern you.
Hadith

The admonition above seems like common sense. It is best to mind your own business, but for the warrior, the question is what *is* his business and what *is not* his business. If you are out buying groceries and on your way back to your car you see some thug trying to mug a lady in the parking lot, is that your business? Many people may consider this whole incident none of their business because they don't want to get involved, but the true warrior doesn't have that option.

Living the warrior lifestyle makes certain things your business, even if you wish that they weren't your business. The situation above is a prime example of this. As a true warrior, you would have an obligation to spring into action to help the lady in trouble. It would be dishonorable for you to simply ignore what was happening to this poor lady in the parking lot. Actually, it is dishonorable for anyone to simply ignore that situation, but that is another subject.

While it is best to leave things alone which don't concern you, it is vital that you are able to discern what concerns you and what does not concern you. "Mind your own business" does not merely mean that you walk through life blindly closing your eyes to the things going on around you. It literally means what it says – *mind* your own business. The personal business of the warrior has a wider range than the personal business of the average person on the street. Think about this.

48

Even if the stream is shallow, wade it as if it were deep.
Korean Proverb

Carelessness is the enemy of the warrior. How much trouble and how many hassles could be avoided if only we would do everything from the attitude expressed in this Korean proverb? The warrior should go about everything that he does both cautiously and confidently at the same time. Even the smallest things should be approached carefully to circumvent the possibility of a simple task turning into a nightmare of a mess. This can happen in the blink of an eye if you are not careful.

Have you ever had a simple chore to accomplish only to have it turn into this kind of nightmare? For example, maybe you were going to do something as simple as hanging a picture on the wall of your dojo. Instead of taking the time to measure, drill the hole, and use the correct hardware for the job, you hurried and decided to just hammer in a nail to hang the picture. In your haste, you made a hole in the wall that had to be repaired. Suddenly a very simple task has cost you much more time and work.

Wouldn't it have been better to slow down and take the time to do the chore correctly? Always approach everything that you do with an attitude of doing the best that you can do. Remember the old saying, if it is worth doing it is worth doing right. A little caution can save you a big headache. No matter how simple or easy the task at hand may be, it is important to perform that task with quality in mind. Keep in mind, haste makes waste. Slow down and make quality your signature.

49

In whatever position you find yourself, determine first your objective.
Marshall Ferdinand Foch

Your objective is your goal or your purpose. As you may already know, in order for you to hit your target, you must first know what your target is. This is common sense. The first step in achieving your goal is knowing what your goal is. Without knowing what your goal or objective is, how would you determine what needs to be done in order to reach your objective. Different objectives require different actions in order to successful.

This principle applies to everything that you do. The first step in any endeavor should be to determine your objective. This is particularly important to the warrior and yet another of the traits which sets the warrior apart from the man who is only a street fighter. The street fighter will not let an insult go unnoticed or unaddressed. His foolish pride will not let such an offense slide. He has a warped sense of honor which tells him that he must put this guy in his place.

The true warrior, on the other hand, takes into account his objective in this situation. Is his objective to save face, or is his objective to keep himself and those under his care safe in this situation? I think you know the answer. Knowing what his situation is, he knows what his response must be. Different objectives require different responses. It is only when you know what your objective is that you can know what your action should be, and once you have determined your objective, the appropriate actions are much easier to discern.

50

Better be proficient in one art than a smatterer in a thousand.
Japanese Proverb

Many martial artists today like to brag about their varied "resume" of different styles of martial arts that they have practiced. They will talk at length about how they spent this much time practicing Kenpo and this much time practicing Ninjutsu. They take pains to impress you by stating that they even spent three months working out with a mixed martial arts professional and also learned all the "in's and out's" of mixed martial arts. Oh how impressive all their skills seem, until you realize this person really has little skill in any art.

Some people will try to move from one martial art to another without ever having become proficient in the first martial art. Either their attention span is short or their over-inflated ego makes them think that they are so great that they can master any art in months and move on to their next conquest. This can be a dangerous position to be in if they are ever in a situation where they will need their martial arts "skills" during a physical encounter.

It is truly a bad time to realize that you never became proficient in any one art, when you are accosted by two thugs in a dark parking lot. The guy in this example would be much better off had he simply stuck with his original art until he became proficient in it. His "impressive resume" of different styles will not help him when two thugs, with no training at all, mop up the sidewalk with his face. Stay focused and become skilled in one art before moving on to another. Remember why you are training in the first place.

51

Would you persuade,
speak of interest, not of reason.
Benjamin Franklin

The majority of people in this world are focused on what is best for them personally, not on reason. For this reason, if you want to persuade someone to see things from your point of view, or to join you in some endeavor, you should approach them from the standpoint of "what's in it for them," not "why you want them to do it." There is a big difference between these two approaches in the other person's mind. As I have said before, winning is in the details.

When you are approaching someone from their point of view, which is "why should I do this, what's in it for me," their mind is more open to what you are saying. You are speaking about something of value to them. When you approach them from a standpoint of reason, they most likely will not be as open. We live in a "what's in it for me" society for the most part. Common sense and reason are lacking, and thus not widely understood.

Some people have a hard time appealing to other's self-interest. It sticks in their craw that people will not listen to reason, but this is another good example that shows why you must be aware of your overall objective. Is your objective to be right and prove the other person wrong, or is your overall objective to persuade the other person to see things from your point of view? Remember, adapt your actions and tactics to your objectives, not the other way around. Focus on accomplishing your objective, and learn the art of persuasion.

52

What you wish others to do, do yourself.
Ramakrishna

The Golden Rule is found throughout the world in basically every culture and in the wisdom writings from the sages of every age. Although it is stated a little differently from place to place, the underlying meaning remains the same – treat others like you want to be treated. This version by Ramakrishna, while one of the ones that is worded slightly differently, is saying the same thing. Your actions should be the same actions that you would like from others.

If you wish that others would live a life of honor, integrity, and character, then you should be living that kind of life yourself. If you are a true warrior, you are already integrating these traits into your life, or at least you should be. We all know that the Golden Rule says for you to do unto others as you would have them do unto you, but there is one subtlety that most people overlook. It says what you should do; it doesn't mention any give and take, such as do unto others, if they are nice to you.

As a true warrior, you are responsible for your actions regardless of how anyone else acts. If they act like a rude, tactless idiot; it doesn't matter. You are still responsible for living by the standards of the warrior lifestyle. If they return your compassion and benevolence with nastiness and malevolence, that is their shortcoming. Your focus has to remain on how *you* should act. Don't let the actions of others determine whether or not you will live up to your own code of conduct. Remain true to your own standards.

53

It is necessary to the happiness of man that he be mentally faithful to himself.
Thomas Paine

The warrior won't be happy if he does not live according to the standards which he has decided to live by, standards which are in line with the lifestyle of the warrior. His conscience will not allow him to live in peace if he is constantly breaking his code of honor in his dealings with others. It seems that the majority of people can lie, cheat or steal and go on with their lives without giving their actions a second thought, but it is not that way for the man who is a warrior at heart.

Warriors do not just live according to their standards and code of ethics when it is convenient or when they think about it. The code of the warrior is ingrained in his soul; it is a part of who he truly is inside. If he is not mentally faithful to himself and the code which is a part of his life, he will not be at peace, and the man who is not at peace with himself will find that he is not happy. Oh, he may seem happy on the outside, but inside, where it truly counts, he will be in turmoil.

Once you know beyond a doubt that you want to travel the path of the warrior, and you have made a decision about the kind of person that you want to be, you must live up to that decision. There is no compromise where your code of honor is concerned. The warrior's conscience is his true guide and there is no room for compromise. Don't assume that you can do "it" just this once and then forget about "it." The conscience of the warrior has a long memory and is unforgiving until things are put right. Think about this.

54

Neither anger nor fear
shall find lodging in your mind.
Dekanawidah

I have written about the need to always stay in control of your emotions. This is especially true for those who seek to live the lifestyle of the warrior. The warrior realizes that he cannot allow himself to be influenced by negative emotions such as anger and fear, but Dekanawidah, the author of the Great Law of the Iroquois Confederacy, takes this truism one step further. He goes as far as to say that you should not even allow these emotions to find lodging in your mind.

At first this quote seems obvious. Of course you shouldn't allow anger and fear to remain in your mind. You cannot afford to hang on to all the negative emotions that pop into your mind over time. This would have a negative impact on your health, both mentally and physically. But is this really what Dekanawidah is saying here? If we look closer, the admonition takes on a more serious connotation. The word lodging actually means a temporary place to stay.

So when we look at the literal definition of this word, we see that we should not even dwell on our anger or fear for a short while. We should not even provide them a place in our mind overnight. These emotions must be acknowledged when they manifest themselves and then they should be dealt with quickly. Don't cultivate them. Don't give them time to grow. Simply realize that they are there, and then turn to your rational thought processes and deal with them appropriately. Self-control is the key.

55

We should live as though our life would be both long and short.
Bias

At first this quote by Bias seems like an oxymoron, but it's really not. Think about how you would live your life if you knew that you were going to die in one or two months. What things would you do? What business would you make sure was taken care of before you died? Would you get your finances straight? Maybe you would take steps to make sure that your family is provided for, or that any old feelings of resentment were resolved. There are probably many things that you would want to take care of before you died.

Now think about how you should live if you knew that you were going to live to be 105 years old. Would you prepare for the future by making sure that you and your family would be taken care of and would have plenty for the years to come? Would you try to make strong, lasting friendships with quality people who you would spend time with throughout the years? Would you study to improve your life? Would you take care of your health so that your body would be healthy and strong while you live?

What Bias is saying is that you should do both. Make sure that all of these things are taken care of now. Live like you are going to be here for many, many years, but at the same time put your life in order now in case your time is short. Don't procrastinate. If there are certain things which you know need to be taken care of us now – do them now. Invest for the future in every way, spiritually, mentally, physically, and financially. Do it now. Remember that no matter how long your life is, it is still short.

56

We must not be innocents abroad in a world that is not innocent.
George Washington

Naivete can get you killed. Many people live their lives in a Pollyanna style haze. They live in their own little world where they never have to encounter the realities of the ugly side of life. They never come into contact with evil, and therefore they have their doubts whether it even exists. When they see signs of it on the news, they justify it by blaming it on poverty or abuse or whatever, from the comfort of their own little fortress, feeling secure that, "That kind of thing could never happen to my family."

And most of them live their lives without coming in direct contact with the other world, this dark underworld where morals and standards are as different from their own as night is from day. The problem is that these people carry their naïve view of the world with them when they leave the security of their world and venture out into new territories. This is very dangerous. They enter a world that they neither understand nor are prepared to encounter, and they do so blindly.

As George Washington pointed out many years ago, you must not be an innocent sheep in a world of wolves. He also stated that you must be ready for conflict at all times. The real world, as sad as it may be, is not a world of innocent people, all caring about the welfare of others. There are bad people out there, some of them REALLY BAD, and they will not take pity on you because of your innocence, in fact they see your innocence as an invitation to attack. If you are going to play in the jungle, you should understand the predator.

57

For one word a man is often deemed to be wise, and for one word he is often deemed to be foolish.
Confucius

Public opinion is fickle. The public, and people in general, are swayed by the way things seem, not the way things truly are. It does not take much to elevate yourself into the good graces of the public, and it takes even less for them to turn against you like a pack of wolves. One good, inspiring speech and everyone thinks that you are an amazingly wise man, but the second that you make a mistake and say something that rubs people the wrong way, your name is mud. Even in Confucius' time this was true.

There are many examples of this fact in our world today. A man can be the biggest celebrity in Hollywood. Paparazzi will follow him all over just to get a photograph of him. He is invited to all the right parties. Everyone wants to interview him. He commands millions of dollars to do a movie. But just let him make one mistake and say something racially or religiously biased, and suddenly he is scorned by the masses. He is finished, and by his own words.

This is why it is important for the warrior to carefully consider every word that comes out of his mouth. Nothing can ruin your good reputation quicker than your own uncontrolled tongue. One careless word in the wrong company can destroy the reputation that it took you years to build. Be a wise man and think before you speak. Consider your words and the possible consequences of what you are thinking of saying before you say it. Don't be foolish.

58

There are more bad men than good.
Francesco Guicciardini

The above sentiment is repeated over and over by sages throughout history. At first this statement seems false. How could there be more bad men than good? Wouldn't that mean that our world would be in chaos? Well, it depends on several factors, one being how you define a good man. If a good man is defined by the qualities that are an integral part of the warrior lifestyle, then there are definitely more bad men than good men. It is rare to find someone who truly lives by real, definable standards of honor.

I think that Guicciardini was actually thinking of three categories of men when he wrote this – bad men, good men, and average men. The average man, while he may not have the stringent qualities that the warrior lives his life by, is not an evil man. He simply goes through life doing what he perceives to be the best thing for himself and his family. Sometimes his decisions go awry because he does not have a set code of ethics on which to base his decisions. His ethics, actions and decisions are situational and fluid.

This leaves two groups: men of excellence (good men) and truly bad men. It is pretty obvious that there are more bad men in this world than men who take honor seriously. Our jails are full of them, tens of thousands of them, while at the same time, it is fairly rare to run into a man who lives by the principles of the warrior lifestyle. Because there are many more bad men than good men, the warrior must be alert and aware of the actions of those around him. You have a much greater chance of running into a bad man than a man of honor.

59

The pebble in the brook secretly thinks itself a precious stone.
Japanese Proverb

No one likes to feel inferior to someone else. This little gem of wisdom is one that should be filed under "good to know" in the warrior's mental files. Because the true warrior is a man of excellence, it can be natural that others may feel inferior in his presence unless he makes a conscious effort to make them feel at ease. I have talked with many men who I consider to be true warriors and they have actually confided in me that it seems as if other people are intimidated when they are in their presence.

Superior men radiate a certain type of energy. A person in the presence of a true warrior can sense this energy, and although they can't really explain what it is that they are sensing, they can sense that there is something special about this man. Most, it seems, sense this energy and are slightly intimidated by the warrior's presence. To them, they don't really know why, but they feel that this man is not someone to cross; they feel that he would be a force to be reckoned with and that he should be treated with respect.

Though the true warrior is a man of humility as well as honor, he has to remember that others will sense this energy and may well be intimidated by him. He must also remember that even the lowest of the low secretly think that they are something special. Almost no one truly thinks deep in his heart that he is beneath most men. Everyone secretly thinks that he or she is special, no matter what the ugly truth may be. The warrior is a finely cut diamond in a brook full of river rocks which secretly think that they are rubies and emeralds.

60

When the time comes that foes pose as friends, keep a friendly face but banish their brotherhood from your heart.
Tiruvalluvar

Things change constantly, and this includes your acquaintances and those who would like to see you destroyed. People, who you once considered your enemies, may later reconcile and offer their hand in friendship. Be careful when this happens. I'm not suggesting that you should be unfriendly or hold a grudge, but you should definitely not consider those people true friends whom you would confide in and take into your confidence.

While you should always conduct yourself with courtesy, it is unwise to think that a leopard will change its spots. A previous enemy may outwardly seek to be on friendly terms with you, but it is likely that he will still hold resentments deep in his heart where you are concerned. Be on friendly terms if you wish, but always be aware of what information you share with this person, and don't put too much trust in what this person says or does.

Consider a reconciled foe as an acquaintance, not a friend. There is a big difference in the two. Don't hold resentments against this person, but at the same time don't be naïve and think that he now has your best interest at heart either. Forgive, but do not forget. This does not mean that you should dwell on what happened in the past, only that you should keep that information filed away in your mental computer for later reference if needed. Be careful not to be conned; enemies have many deceptive ways to hurt you.

61

Method is more important than strength, when you wish to control your enemies.
Nagarjuna

At some point and time your strength will wane; this is just part of growing older. You can't always depend on your strength to get you out of every situation that you may encounter when it comes to dealing with your enemies, especially in today's world where your enemies are just as likely, if not more so, to attack you in ways other than physically. Remember that your enemy is not always going to be some street thug. There are many others that may seek to injure you, and in more underhanded ways.

Although it is very important for the warrior to keep his martial arts skills well-honed, it is just as important that he maintains his other self-defense skills as well. Your mind will always be your first and best line of defense. Method and strategy will defeat strength. When you want to control your enemies, you must employ many other advantages besides physical superiority. Having physical superiority will not protect you from non-physical and unconventional attacks.

Stay alert to attacks on your character or your reputation. Expect your enemy to attack you through the backdoor, not face to face. The warrior will not have enemies who are men of honor, character and integrity, but rather enemies who have very little integrity at all. These types of men have no code of honor and will do anything and everything to obtain what they want. Realize that this is their character. Expect a snake to act like a snake, and be ready when he strikes.

62

In hardship you know your friends.
Japanese Proverb

The term "fair weather friend" is a fairly common term which is used to describe so-called friends who are only your "friend" when it is convenient for them. It is common wisdom, throughout the world, that you only truly know who your true friends are when times are rough. Real friends are known during hard times. They are the ones who don't turn their back on you when your back is against the wall, even if it means they must roll up their sleeves and fight side by side with you against overwhelming odds.

Without the trials and tribulations of hard times, it is hard to tell who is truly your friend, and who is nothing more than an acquaintance. You may think that someone is your true friend, but do you really know this person? Do you know what is really in this person's heart? Would you trust your life or the lives of your family to this person? These are all questions which must be meditated on when it comes to evaluating whether or not someone is a true friend.

When push comes to shove, your true friends rise above the others and come to your side, ready for battle just as if your problems were their problems. They come to you ready to meet Goliath head on, willing to play it out to the end, whether that means doing a victory dance at the end of the day, or using each other as a crutch to limp on back home after Goliath kicks both of your butts. To him, the outcome does not matter; what matters is that he was there, shoulder to shoulder with you when you needed him most.

63

Kill the spider and you will destroy the cobweb.
Maltese Proverb

Everything in life is governed by the principle of cause and effect. Nothing happens without a reason, even if you don't know what that reason may happen to be. Whether you call it karma or the law of reciprocity, one thing always leads to another. Everything in your life has some cause behind it which brought it about. There is nothing that you can do which does not have some accompanying effect. If you don't like the results that you have been getting, change the actions that brought about those results.

This is the wisdom behind this Maltese Proverb. If you don't like cobwebs, get rid of the spider. When you kill the spider, there will be no more cobwebs, at least not from that specific spider. If you simply remove the cobweb itself, the spider will only spin more of them, and the cycle will continue endlessly, until you finally address the underlying cause – the spider. When you remove the primary cause, the effect will cease to exist.

This same principle applies to any problem that you may have in your life. If you can figure out what the underlying cause is for that specific problem, you can make a rational decision concerning how to eliminate that cause, therefore getting rid of the problem. Remove the root and the weed will cease to exist. If you don't like the results that you have been getting, change what you have been doing and do something different. Different actions bring about different results.

64

Nothing is less worthy of honor than an old man who has no other evidence of having lived long except his age.

Seneca

Many teachings of the sages state that with age comes wisdom, but that is not necessarily true. Wisdom should come with age, that is a fact, but many times it doesn't. Just as a marksman does not hit the target simply by loading his gun and pulling the trigger, you do not acquire wisdom simply by staying alive year after year. You must dig for it and earn it. Focus on it and stay determined to be wise, just as the marksman concentrates and holds his aim steady on his target.

Wisdom does not come automatically with age anymore than hitting the target comes automatically by shooting a gun. Likewise, accomplishments and wisdom do not come automatically because someone has lived a long life. You have to work hard for the things that are worth having in your life. If you have lived a long life and have nothing to show for it other than the fact that you have been able to clothe and feed yourself, where is the honor in that? Can you really say that you have used your life wisely?

I don't think so and neither did Seneca. In fact, Seneca stated that there is nothing less worthy of honor than someone who has lived long, but hasn't done anything with his life. Make it a point in your life to be of use to your fellow man. Do something besides eat, drink and be merry. Help others and be of service. Write, teach, build, impart wisdom, be generous, and help the poor and downtrodden. These are all duties of the true warrior. Live for something bigger than yourself.

65

Listen to your intuition and realilze when the first attack has taken place.
Bohdi Sanders

Action beats reaction. This essentially means that the man who acts first is going to have a considerable advantage over the man who must react to whatever the first man does. If someone has a pistol aimed in your direction, and he is in close range, you may be able to take the pistol away from him before he can pull the trigger, *if* you have the proper training and *if* you act first. But if he decides to act first and pull the trigger, there is no way you can react fast enough to defend against his action.

The man who acts first always has a big advantage. This is something that the warrior should keep in mind. Although there is no "first attack" in karate, that does not mean that you can't act first in a dangerous situation. As I have explained before, the "first attack" in karate does not mean the first punch or kick that is thrown. The "first attack" happens when you realize that the other person means you harm in some way. It could be verbal or it could be something physical without the punch or kick.

Waiting until your aggressor actually throws a kick or a punch could be a mistake, depending on the situation (every situation is unique and different). If you feel threatened and you know that someone has already engaged in the "first attack," then it certainly may be to your advantage to act instead of wait and respond. A surprised enemy is an enemy well on his way to defeat, and listening to your intuition where your actions are concerned gives you a distinct advantage over your opponent.

66

Trust in God, but tie your camel.
Arabian Proverb

There is a story about an old lady who lived in a town where there was a great flood. People all over were stranded and being rescued from the rising waters of the overflowing river. The flood waters had risen so high and so fast that this lady had climbed to the roof of her house to avoid the rising waters. She sat silently on her roof, praying for God to rescue her and get her out of this mess. Soon a boat came by and the man in the boat told her to get in, but she responded, "No thank you. God will rescue me."

Later another rescue boat came by and offered the lady a ride. Once again the lady responded, "No thank you. God will rescue me." The man in the boat argued with her to no avail, and then sped off to help others in need. The water continued to rise and was just a foot from covering the entire roof where the lady sat, when a helicopter flew over and hovered above her rooftop. The chopper pilot drop a ladder and a rescue worker dropped down to help the lady board the chopper, but the lady refused.

For the third time she said, "No thank you. God will save me." The lady drowned as the flood waters overtook her rooftop. When the lady got to Heaven she asked God, "Why didn't you save me? I prayed over and over, and yet you let me drown!" God replied, "I sent you two boats and a helicopter and you refused to do your part. You drowned because you would not act." The moral of the story is obvious; it is good to have faith, but God expects you to do your part. Not even God respects someone who will not take action when action is needed.

67

Quieten your body.
Quieten your mind.
Buddha

Meditation is an important part of the warrior lifestyle. You should take time to sit quietly and calm your body and your mind in order to develop certain qualities that you need to develop on your journey. Science has proven that there are many benefits associated with meditation. These benefits have been known to the sages for thousands of years and now we know that they are more than just myths. Meditation will help the warrior control his emotions, stay calm in the midst of trouble, and develop his intuition.

It is also important to sit quietly and meditate or reflect on your beliefs. This too is a must for the true warrior. Only through reflecting on what you believe and why you believe what you believe, can you truly understand yourself and the standards by which you live. It is vital for the warrior to take time out from his busy schedule, and spend some quiet time contemplating who he truly is, what his code of honor is, and why he lives according to the principles of the warrior lifestyle.

Warriors seem to have a hard time slowing down and just sitting quietly with their thoughts. Most of them would rather be working out or doing something active, but meditation is an important habit for the warrior to develop. The warrior lifestyle has many different components which must be perfected, and spending time in quiet solitude happens to be one of those components. Don't confuse sitting quietly in meditation or internal reflection with doing nothing. There is a big difference.

68

I stumbled over the roots of the tree I had myself planted.
Goethe

Many times we find that we can be our own worst enemies. Whether it is something we do or something that we say, humans in general have a way of causing their own problems with careless words and actions. This is karma in action. When you do this, you don't have to sit and wonder why a certain thing happened, you know. It happened because you said the wrong thing; you should have kept your mouth shut! I see this over and over. People enjoy talking to other people, and inevitably they will say things that they shouldn't.

Once you have said something, there is no taking it back. The cat is out of the bag. This is why you should choose your words carefully and consider your audience. Don't share too much personal information about yourself. It is not anyone else's business. Keep personal things private. Many times we say something to spite someone else. We just feel that we have to put them in their place, but in doing so, we say things that can be used against us at a later time. It is better to be reserved and remain quiet.

Careless actions can be just as damaging to you as careless words. In fact, these two go hand in hand. Your actions can be used against you just as easily as your words. Keep a tight rein on both your actions and your words. Don't give your enemy the ammunition that he needs to hurt you. There are enough obstacles in life without you planting roots that will someday grow up to trip you. Be smart and control your actions and your speech.

69

Depend on others and you will go hungry.
Nepalese Proverb

The warrior should be self-sufficient, at least as much as possible. It is much better for others to depend on you, than for you to have to depend on others for what you need in your life. Dependence on others can put you in a tricky position at times. When you depend on someone else for something, you are giving that person a certain amount of power or control over you, and this is even more true if you have to depend on someone for something important.

It is much better to be self-sufficient. Do what you can to become as self-reliant as possible. Don't leave yourself open to the whims or mercy of others. While it is true that in today's society the majority of us are dependent to a large extent on others, whether it is for your income, your food, your heat, or whatever, not many of us are totally independent. In fact, unless you have your own farm, with your own water supply and food supply, you are not truly self-reliant.

Most people never really think about this point, but the warrior should give thought to the future and to making sure that his family is safe and provided for, no matter what changes occur. Besides buying your own farm and raising your own food, there are many ways that you can make yourself more independent. Do some research on what goes into making someone safe and ready for an emergency situation. Think about what you would need to keep yourself and your family safe should you find your normal sources of food and water are no longer available to you. Be as prepared as possible.

70

Silence is the cornerstone of character.
Ohiyesa

To understand this quote from Ohiyesa, you first have to understand the concept of a cornerstone. The cornerstone is the first stoned laid at a corner of a building where two walls will eventually be built. It forms the first part of a new building, and if it is not level and square, everything that comes after it will be a little off kilter. Essentially it is fundamentally important to the walls, floors, and ceiling. If the cornerstone is not right, nothing else will be right.

According to Ohiyesa, silence is the cornerstone of character. This means that the man who does not understand how to be silent and how to control his tongue will inevitably find that his character will be just a little out of balance. Remember, if the cornerstone is not right, then everything that is built on that cornerstone will be off balance as well. Learning to control your speech and knowing when to be silent is an essential part of being a warrior, as is spending time in silent meditation.

In order for the warrior to understand his code of honor and what he stands for, he must spend time in silence, contemplating his beliefs and his standards. If you skip this part of your training, you will eventually discover the discord in your spirit. Sometimes full speed ahead, is not the fastest way to get where you want to go. You must take the time to slow down, be silent, and meditate on the path that you have chosen to travel, and to make sure that you are still on your chosen path and have not made an unintentional detour.

71

There is nothing on this earth more to be prized than true friendship.
Saint Thomas of Aquinas

If you have one true friend, you are rich whether you know it or not. Most people will claim that they have many friends, when in fact they don't have any friends at all. What most people call friends are nothing more than acquaintances. These days, friendship means little more to the average person than someone who he has met or someone with whom he is on a first name basis. This is not what the sages and teachers of old meant when they referred to true friendship.

True friendship goes much deeper than simply knowing someone's name or being acquainted with them; it means that you have someone who will be there for you no matter what. Come hell or high water, a true friendship will endure and thrive. A true friend will be honest with you. He will point out your weaknesses in private, and praise your strengths in public. He will have your back when you need him to, and will be at your side when the stakes are high.

If you are lucky enough to develop a true friendship during your lifetime, you will find that true friendship is indeed worth more than anything else on this earth. You may be wondering how you know the difference in a true friend and someone who is simply a buddy. The answer lies in troubled times. The sages taught that it is in times of trouble that your true friends reveal themselves. Anyone is willing to stand beside you when they incur no risk, but only a true friend is willing to put his neck on the line for you.

72

Feel your confidence and see yourself winning. Always see yourself winning.
Loren Christensen

Visualization is an important form of training for the warrior, and very effective if it is done right. Actually, visualization works whether it is done right or wrong. It will produce results either way. The difference is the kind of results which is produced by your visualization practice. If you visualize yourself screwing up, allowing fear to get the best of you, or visualize yourself losing a fight, those exercises will produce results in your life, although they probably won't be the results you want.

As Loren Christensen stated in his wonderful book, *Solo Training 2*, you should always visualize yourself winning. You want to see yourself responding to the various situations with confidence and strength. See yourself as the confident, wise, and rational hero which has command of every situation that he finds himself in, no matter what. Visualization practice is meant to be a form of training. Practice does not make perfect, *perfect* practice makes perfect. Visualize yourself winning with your actions and your words.

Just as you would not want to practice your physical techniques in the dojo incorrectly over and over, you don't want to perform your mental exercises incorrectly over and over. Practicing your techniques incorrectly reinforces bad habits which will eventually become natural for you. The same principle applies to your visualization. If you see yourself in your mind's eye choking during a fight or becoming nervous and making a mistake, what do you think that reinforces? Always see yourself as strong, wise and a winner in every situation.

73

Never admit defeat, even if you have been wounded. The good soldier's wounds spur him to gather his strength.

Desiderius Erasmus

Defeat must not be an option for the warrior. When the time comes that you have to fight for your life or the lives of your loved-ones, there can be no such thing as quitting or giving up. During a life-or-death situation, quitting or giving up means surrendering your life. We aren't talking about a sparring match here, where you need a breather and declare that you have had enough and need a break. There are no "breaks" in a real fight, even if you have been wounded or hurt.

This is something that the warrior must realize *before* he finds himself in that situation, and this is also something that most martial artists do not learn in the dojo. In the dojo the martial artist learns that once a point is scored it is time to stop and go back to the line, or if someone gets hit too hard, they can take a time out to regroup. It isn't like that on the street. You cannot assume that your opponent will be satisfied if he has simply hurt you and you throw in the towel.

On the contrary, on the street this will signal most predators that the fight is almost over and that it is time to really bring on the hurt. If you quit after you are wounded or hurt, you can pretty much count on being injured or hurt much worse, or even killed before the fight is over. Never count on mercy from some street thug, and never admit defeat. If you are in that situation, you cannot afford to stop fighting. Gather your strength and fight through the pain. Defeat is a state of mind. It is not over until you decide that it is over.

74

**Cattle die, and kinsmen die,
And so one dies one's self;
But a noble name will never die,
If good renown one gets.**
The Havamal

The warrior must work to both build and maintain a good reputation. Although he should realize that his reputation is not the most important thing in the world, it is something that he should want to protect, especially once he has worked to attain a good name. I say that it is not the most important thing because, when you are put to the test, it is not so much a good reputation that is important as it is being worthy of a good reputation.

There are many people out there who have a good reputation, but who are totally undeserving of that reputation. Their good name is nothing more than an illusion created by a specific blueprint in a deliberate attempt to mislead people. They aren't men of character and integrity, and their reputation is as counterfeit as a three dollar bill. Men like this have their titles and their positions, but underneath it all, their character is hollow and their good reputation is unwarranted.

On the other hand, there are people who have a bad reputation who are men of upstanding character, that have simply made a mistake or who have had their reputation deliberately tarnished by their enemies. It takes little to tarnish your good name, and this is one of the ways that your enemies will attack you in today's society. Take the time to protect your reputation, but spend even more time making sure that you actually deserve a good reputation.

75

Perception is strong and sight is weak.
Miyamoto Musashi

Always believe in and follow your intuition, even when it does not make sense to you. People are experts at hiding the truth and being deceptive. Many times you will be unable to detect their deception with your physical senses, but your intuition and sense of honor will let you know inside that something just doesn't feel right. While you may not be able to pinpoint the issue, you will sense that something is not right. When you get this feeling, it is time to take a step back and re-evaluate the situation.

The trick to listening to your intuition is slowing down and listening to your spirit. Just as you cannot listen to someone giving a speech, the radio, the television, and your wife, all at the same time, you cannot listen to your intuition when you have too many external things going on at the same time. Take time to be quiet and meditate. You have to intentionally listen to your intuition, just as you must actively listen to someone to really hear what they are saying to you.

Not only do you have to take the time to remove yourself from the external influences which render the voice of your intuition mute, but you also have to learn to trust what you "hear" your intuition tell you. At first this will be more of a feeling, but with practice it will come to you in the form of conscious thoughts. Then the ball is in your court. You must have the confidence in your intuition to act on what it is telling you. This confidence also comes with practice and use. Start using your internal intelligence, and see the unseen.

76

Nothing is better or surer than fixing things in such a way that you are safe, not because your enemy is unwilling, but because he is unable to hurt you.
Francesco Guicciardini

This quote by Francesco Guicciardini, from his great book, *Maxims and Reflections*, should be taken to heart by every warrior. This is what you are training for in your dojo. This quote should be posted in every dojo throughout the country. The warrior should not depend on the goodwill of some thug; that is madness. You can't count on the probability that your enemy is really not motivated enough to truly hurt you, whether physically or in some other way.

This careless attitude offers you no security whatsoever, only a naïve faith in the goodness of those who may not be so good. Instead of hoping that your enemy will be unwilling to hurt you, it is much better to take steps to ensure that he can't hurt you, even if he so desires. Don't leave things up to chance. Fix things so that your enemy is unable to hurt you, then you will have peace of mind and a degree of security that comes with knowing that you are prepared for whatever your enemy may throw at you.

It seems that the majority of people today are doing just the opposite. They are walking around totally unprepared, mindlessly hoping that their enemy or the thug on the street is simply unwilling to hurt them. They live a life of chance. This is not the way of the warrior. The warrior takes pains to ensure that he is ready for whatever he may encounter. Structure your life in a way that you know that you are safe, at least as much as you can. Be prepared.

77

Pardon the other man's faults but deal strictly with your own.
Sai Baba

Confucius taught that the superior man demands it of himself, but the inferior man demands it of others. This can be seen in the attitudes of people today. The majority of people will harshly attack others when they stumble, but they never seem to run out of excuses or justifications for their own actions when it is they who stumble. They do just the opposite of what Sai Baba is teaching in the quote above; they want to deal strictly with the faults of others while at the same time excusing their own bad behavior.

The superior man on the other hand, is more concerned about his own actions than the actions of other people. He is much more willing to pardon the other man's faults than to let his own shortcomings slide. He knows that everyone makes mistakes and he is willing to forgive others when they fall short, but he takes his own actions much more seriously. The warrior actively tries to perfect his character and therefore will not allow his own mistakes to go unaddressed.

His character, integrity and honor are so important to him, that he actually demands more from himself than anyone else expects of him. He holds himself to a higher standard than he expects from others, which is why he is so willing to overlook the faults of other people. The true warrior understands that not everyone lives by the code of the warrior, and therefore he should not be surprised when others don't live according to his high standards. Focus on perfecting your own character, not the character of others.

78

To compose our character is our duty.
Montaigne

Montaigne was not speaking to warriors when he made the statement above, but rather to men in general. If it is the duty of men to compose their character, how much more so is it the duty of the warrior to compose his character and ensure that his character, integrity and honor is above reproach? This should be the main goal for the warrior. He should spend time meditating on his character and his code of honor, and how to best perfect both in his life.

The struggle to perfect your character is an integral part of the warrior lifestyle; in fact it is the most important part. Character, integrity and honor are what set the warrior apart from the ordinary man or the street thug for that matter. It is not the fact that he is trained in certain martial arts skills or that he has a passion for the fighting arts. Many people have a passion for martial arts and know how to fight who are nowhere close to being true warriors.

What sets the true warrior apart from the thug and the average man is his focus on developing his character to the best of his ability. This does not mean that he is perfect or that he will not fall short of his lofty ideals. Everyone has set backs from time to time while struggling with their own personal demons. What this does mean is that we do not simply give in to our demons. The warrior does not simply throw in the towel when he slips and falls. He perseveres and continues to work at perfecting his character.

79

Great spirits have always encountered violent opposition from mediocre minds.
Albert Einstein

Don't expect everyone to see the value in your quest to live the warrior lifestyle. People who do not respect the qualities of integrity, character and honor, will most likely not respect your decision to live by warrior values. They don't see the value in living a life of excellence or aspiring to high ideals. To them it is folly to live according to a code of standards which puts honor ahead of profit, comfort, or personal gain. Most people's first concern is what is "best" for them.

It never enters their mind that maybe the best thing for them is to live by a code of honor. Sometimes making profits or being comfortable is not really what is best for you. The warrior realizes that it is always best in the long run to make your decisions according to your code of honor, even if those decisions cost you a business deal or some profits. It never profits you to go against your standards, even if it seems like it will. All of the sages taught this truth, but few people today understand the reality of it.

This realization only comes through deep reflection on the value of your code of honor. The warrior understands this and makes time to really reflect on his standards. He realizes that he is a man of excellence, a great spirit, and that those with mediocre minds will not understand his way of life. For this reason, he is careful with whom he discusses his code of honor. He knows that the majority of people will belittle his goal of perfection of character as simple arrogance. Expect opposition and excel anyway.

80

Ordinary people are friendly with those who are outwardly similar to them. The wise are friendly with those who are inwardly similar to them.
Lieh Tzu

Most people will look at someone who has the same hobbies or pastimes as they do and be drawn toward them because they appear similar to each other. This is a very natural human trait. When someone seems to have interests in common with you, you find it easy to relate to them. If Joe likes martial arts, and you are a black belt, then the two of you automatically have that shared interest.

But what this Taoist scripture is saying is that this is how the "ordinary" man looks at others. He is friendly to those who share external interests and qualities. The wise man, in our case, the warrior, should seek the companionship of those who are inwardly similar to them. This does not mean that you shouldn't seek friendship with those who have the same external interest as you, but it means that you should consider their internal qualities to be of more importance than their external qualities.

What is the difference in external qualities and internal qualities? Well, an example of an external quality would be a passion for the martial arts, whereas an internal quality would be someone who values integrity and honor. What you really want in your friends is someone who has both, someone who enjoys the same things as you do, but at the same time is also a person of character, integrity and honor. This does not mean that all your friends have to be martial artists, but they should all be people of honor.

81

One kind word warms
three winter months.
Japanese Proverb

I have already discussed, many times, how the warrior should mind his tongue and watch what he says to other people. It is vital that he does not defeat himself or destroy his reputation with thoughtless and careless words uttered in times of stress or anger. All of the sages taught the importance of this concept, and how easy it is to allow a few seconds of uncontrolled anger to destroy friendships and reputations. I have discussed this at length in all three of my *Warrior Wisdom* books.

But one aspect of your speech that I have not spent a lot of time writing about is the flip side of this coin. While it is true that the warrior is a man of few words, and that you have to be careful not to allow your mouth to get you into trouble, it is also true that you can do great good with your speech if you set your mind to it. It is part of the warrior's duty to serve and help others, and this is a simple but profound way to do so, and to make a great impact with little effort.

You never know how much a kind word or some sound advice will help someone who is in need. It is impossible to know just how far the ripples that one kind word will travel or the changes that it may cause in someone's life. The sincere compliment, which you give someone who is down and out, may be the one thing that stands between that person and suicide. The advice that you give to a new martial arts student may be the difference between him quitting the martial arts and his dedication to the warrior lifestyle.

82

It's not the skill to win, but the will to win.

Alain Burrese

Your martial arts skills can take you a long way in a physical conflict. Training is important. You have to be proficient in the art of self-defense, especially when you find yourself confronted by an experienced street fighter who is set on rearranging your face. The dedication that you have to your training today may save your life tomorrow. When it comes down to it, this is what Gichin Funakoshi meant by taking your training deadly serious.

While it is very true that you must take your training seriously, and you must develop your skills to a high level in order to be able to protect yourself and those around you, all of this is useless without the will to win. A hard punch to the nose has a way of separating those with a strong will to survive, from those who will quickly throw in the towel. This is when the will of the warrior comes into play. You must have that "never give up" spirit in order to survive in a real street confrontation.

Your "will" is basically the inner part of you which consciously makes the decision about what you will and will not do. It is your overall determination. You have to determine that you will not quit, that you will walk away from the fight victorious. Any other outcome is not acceptable. You cannot expect mercy on the street. Without the will to win, you had better not get caught up in a real street fight, because you will be in trouble. Add the will to win with your martial skills, and you will have a winning combination.

83

He who wants to sell his honor will always find a buyer.
Arabian Proverb

Your honor doesn't mean anything to anyone else besides you. Nobody else cares if you compromise your values. It makes no difference to them. Remember, most people are only interested in themselves; they aren't concerned with your integrity or your honor. If you are willing to compromise your honor to go along with the crowd or to please others, they will certainly oblige you.

If you are willing to sell your honor, no matter what the price, you will find someone willing to accommodate you. There will always be someone, somewhere, who will have just the right temptation to entice you to barter your honor. Your honor has to be firm in order to be worth anything. Honor that is not unyielding is not honor at all, but rather someone's false sense of honor. Real honor has no price and cannot be tempted by the whims of other people.

The warrior should have a code of honor that is set in stone. Your honor should not be for sale at any price. If your honor is not built on a firm foundation, it will be in danger of crumbling at some time, even if it looks solid from the viewpoint of the world. Things have to be right on the inside before they can be right on the outside. You can paint termite infested walls and they will look good, but it is only cosmetic. Sooner or later that rotten core will collapse. Think about this.

84

When you shoot an arrow of truth, dip its point in honey.
Arabian Proverb

There is absolutely no reason for intentionally hurting someone's feelings and using the truth as an excuse for doing so, or for being tactless and justifying such action by declaring that you were only speaking the truth. While it is true that you should be truthful, there is always a way to be truthful without being abrasive. Speaking the truth does not justify being rude and tactless, although being rude does say something about your lack of judgment. You must always carefully think about what you are going to say before you say it.

As a warrior, you have a responsibility to be truthful, but at the same time you have a responsibility to be wise and to consider the outcome of your actions. This includes the consequences of what you say. Some people think that if something is true, they should just speak their mind regardless of the consequences. After all, it doesn't matter if it hurts someone if it is true, right? Wrong!

You must be wise enough to be able to speak the truth without causing hard feelings. Have you actually accomplished anything by putting someone on the defensive or by causing them to resent you? Will their anger towards you have a positive effect on their life? These are things that you should consider when you speak. A little tact goes a long way and can come much closer to achieving your objective than an abrasive approach. Use some discretion and diplomacy. Think before you speak.

85

You can't please everybody.
Aesop

We have all heard this aphorism many times, and it is still as true today as when Aesop wrote it in his famous fables. You will never please everybody no matter how hard you try. I have been called every name in the book for some of the articles that I have written. I have been called a sage and an idiot, a Democrat and a Republican, a pagan and a Christian, all from the same article! Yes, these people all read the exact same article and yet people's perceptions of the article, and of me, ranged from love to hate.

The warrior understands the wisdom behind this aphorism and does not try to please everyone. In fact, he is not that concerned about pleasing anyone. His focus is on doing what is right, and fulfilling his duty according to his code of honor. He does what is his to do and does not concern himself with the opinions of others, realizing that most people simply do not understand the warrior lifestyle. Not all people are equal, and not everyone's opinion really matters.

This is another truism that the warrior thoroughly understands. There are people whom he looks up to and whose opinions matter to him, but these are not the common men. These are men of honor, men who understand wisdom and integrity, and who, like the warrior, seek to live a life of excellence. It is these men's opinions that truly matter to the warrior, not the opinions of lesser men. You can't please everybody, but if you find that men of honor are constantly displeased with your actions, it is time for some introspection.

86

The warrior backs up his words with conviction and action.
Tony L. Jones

It may seem to many of my readers that I spend a great deal of time considering the importance of exercising diplomacy when speaking, and I do. There is a simple reason for this, your mouth can get you into more trouble, faster than anything else that I know of, and it doesn't have to be that way. There is a simple solution to this potentially dangerous problem – think before you speak, and mean what you say. Although this is a pretty simple way to stay safe, at least where this one danger is concerned, it is easier said than done.

Controlling your urge to give someone a severe tongue lashing can be a challenge. It is all too easy to vent your anger and say things that you neither mean nor would have the conviction to back up if you did mean them. This is an area where the warrior has to constantly monitor himself, especially when he is upset or angry. Anger has a way of escaping in the form of nasty, hurtful words, which later require apologies and which will probably cause you future problems.

The warrior has to defeat his personal temptations to put someone in his place. One way to do this is to remember that your words should mean something, that you want people to see you as a man of your word, not some hothead who allows his anger to dictate his speech. There is no way to back up your words with conviction and action if you allow yourself to spew out emotional garbage, filled with anger. In order to back up your words with conviction and action, they must be calm and rational. Think about this.

87

To be a samurai is to be polite at all times.
Hojo Nagauji

The samurai were expected to conduct themselves with honor and a sense of civility at all times. Politeness was a part of their way of life, probably because the teachings of Confucius were commonly studied by the samurai, and conducting yourself with civility and appropriateness is a common theme throughout the teachings of Confucius. A samurai took his behavior with others seriously and this included being polite and acting with benevolence.

Like the samurai of old, the modern day warrior should strive to develop a sense of civility in his actions and dealings with others. Don't lower yourself to the current standards of the day which put little or no importance on manners. It seems that in today's society, it is fairly rare to encounter a young person who understands the importance of manners and politeness. The list of character traits which set the warrior apart from the common person continues to grow.

The man of excellence will exhibit that excellence in the way that he treats others. The fact that those around him do not deserve to be treated in a polite manner, or that they are completely rude and obnoxious, does not deter the superior man from being a man of excellence. He acts as he should, regardless of the actions of others. He treats others with politeness because that is who he is, not because of what or who they are. Your mannerisms say something about who you are as a person, not about those around you; who they are, or are not, is irrelevant. What matters is that you conduct yourself as you should.

88

The true victory is
defeat of your base nature.
Gojun Miyagi

During his journey on the path of the warrior, the warrior will have many opportunities to win countless victories, both externally and internally. Some of those victories will be quick and decisive and others will be tougher and ongoing. The victory which Gojun Miyagi is speaking of in the above quote is the victory over yourself. It is the fight to perfect your character, and is a recurring daily fight. This is one encounter which the warrior cannot walk away from, for it will follow him wherever he goes.

There is no ignoring this foe in hopes that he will decide that an encounter with you is simply not worth it. This antagonist, your base nature, will never tire; it will never take a day off to rest. This enemy is always waiting to ambush you when you are at your weakest point. You can't afford to lower your guard or this opponent will find a way to slip a solid blow in under your defenses. There is no truce with this foe; there is only constant battle, surrender, or victory.

It seems that most people lose this war and surrender to this enemy, but the warrior is not in the habit or surrendering. He knows that this enemy stands between him and the fulfillment of his goal – the perfection of his character. Therefore he does not merely sit back and shield himself from the attacks of his base nature. Instead, he actively takes the battle to this foe and destroys him with no mercy. Total victory is all that the warrior will settle for in this case, and in doing so he wins a true and lasting victory.

89

A hundred lifetimes may not be enough to rectify the mistake made in one short morning.
Chinese Proverb

It takes a long time to build a reputation of being a man of honor and integrity. Building your reputation is something that you have to work at continuously. You cannot afford to let your guard down when it comes to your character. It takes a lot of effort, forethought, and determination, to not only build a good reputation, but to make that reputation true – to walk the walk, and not just talk the talk. Those who only talk the talk are soon found out.

While it can take a lifetime to build your reputation, it may only take minutes to destroy it. Like many things, it is much easier to obliterate your reputation than it is to build it. A good analogy would be finishing a beautiful room in your home. It takes a lot of thought, material, planning, and labor to finish a room in your home. The walls must be measured and built to certain standards. Then they have to be covered and painted. A lot of time and money goes into the final product.

It can take weeks to finish the walls for one room, but think about how fast those same walls can be destroyed by one unskilled buffoon with a sledgehammer. It takes very little to ruin what took many hours to build. The same principle applies to your reputation. It takes thought, planning, and work to build a good reputation, but it can be completely destroyed in just a few quick minutes by thoughtless actions. Be careful to maintain the character and reputation that you have worked so hard to build.

90

A promise is a debt.
Irish Proverb

Many people make promises without any consideration for their words. Their word is absolutely meaningless to them. A promise from them is to be taken with a grain of salt. It usually means little more than they are in a desperate state at the time and they are willing to say anything to get whatever it is that they need for the moment. Once they have what they are after, their promise is quickly forgotten. They never consider that a promise is a debt, after all, who is going to force them to live up to their word?

The warrior, on the other hand, is a man of his word. If he promises that he will do something, he does it, period. He doesn't make empty promises just to get his way, this would be dishonorable. He takes his word of honor seriously. To him, a promise is indeed a debt, and a debt that will be repaid. Warriors feel honor bound to make their word good. People who make empty promises lose the respect of those around them, and the warrior realizes this.

He is not willing to compromise his word or the respect that his character affords him. To the man of honor, a promise means as much as a written contract that is signed and notarized. His word is good whether it is written on paper or written on the wind. Your promise is your word of honor. It should not matter whether or not your promise is legally binding in a court of law. The warrior lives by a higher law than the law of the land; he lives by the law of honor.

91

However troubled the times, men of imperturbable perception never commit shameful or sordid deeds.
Tiruvalluvar

As I write this, the current state of the economy in our country is not good. In fact, it is pretty bad and getting worse by the day. The other day I saw a piece on the news which stated that there is a huge increase in the amount of shoplifting throughout the country. The reporter stated that this increase has to do with the fact that the economy is bad and people are "forced" to do things that they wouldn't otherwise do, such as steal from other people. Oh really? The economy is "forcing" these people to become thieves?

If that theory were true, why aren't all people who are having a hard time in this economy turning to crime? This is the same excuse that we hear when there is a power outage in the cities and people run wild and loot the stores. We are told that it is simply because of poverty, and that these people are simply pushed to their limit. I have another theory. My theory is that these are people of low character, period. Their thievery is not result of the economy or their poverty, but rather the result of their lack of honor.

As Tiruvalluvar stated, men of honor do not turn to thief, murder, looting, or any other shameful deeds simply because of troubled times. Troubled times are simply an excuse or a justification for the shortcoming in these people's character. The warrior's actions are rooted in honor, integrity and justice, and he will not lower his standards and then blame his actions on anything or anybody else.

92

The superior man must always remain himself in all situations of life.
Chung Yung

One of the traits of the true warrior is the ability to meet a variety of stressful and even dangerous situations in life without losing his head. He is able to remain calm, cool and collected no matter what life throws at him. He has the ability to remain true to his character, integrity and honor through the many temptations and irritations that he meets on his journey. According to Chung Yung, this is also a trait of the superior man, but as we have already discussed, the warrior and the superior man are one and the same.

How is the warrior able to "always remain himself in all situations?" Does this simply happen naturally because he is a warrior at heart or is this something that he must work at and develop over time? I think that you know the answer to that. This is yet another skill which takes time and effort to perfect. You have to develop the ability to remain calm under stressful situations, it does not come naturally.

Techniques such as meditation, realistic training scenarios, visualization techniques, and specific breathing exercises can all play a part in developing this skill. Courage is also an essential part of remaining true to yourself no matter what the external circumstances. It takes courage to remain true to your convictions and to stand up for what is right. Remain true to your code, to who you have decided to be, and to how you have decided to live your life – no matter what life throws at you.

93

Those who do not learn the lesson of history are doomed to repeat its mistakes.
Herodotus

This quote by Herodotus is often repeated throughout our country today, mostly in connection with war or politics, but it also has meaning for the warrior and the martial artist. As I have said many times, the warrior is not perfect. He, like everyone else, is going to make mistakes. That is just part of life. What is important is that the warrior learns from his mistakes so that he does not repeat the same mistake over and over again. Although his mistakes may not be ancient history, he still must learn lessons from them.

Not only must he learn from his own mistakes and make adjustments where adjustments are needed, but he also should learn from both the mistakes of others and the lessons of history as a whole. Be aware and watch the actions of others in order to learn from their mistakes and their successes. There is something to be learned from the life of everyone that you meet. Look at their actions and learn what should be done and what should not be done.

You can also learn from the mistakes that men have made throughout history. History is not just a collection of dates and facts that you memorize to pass your history class in school. Instead of viewing history in that manner, see history as an opportunity to be able to view the mistakes and successes that other men have made, and learn from what they did. It is ridiculous to make the same mistakes over and over again, when you have the chance to avoid them altogether. Learn lessons from the elders, past and present.

94

The character of every act depends on the circumstances in which it is done.
Oliver Wendell Holmes

Many times when people read this quote by Oliver Wendell Holmes, they automatically think that this is situational ethics and that it flies in the face of true honor. But true honor is not black and white, and this quote has nothing to do with situational ethics. The character, the qualities which make something right or wrong, of every act depends on both the circumstances in which it is done and the intention behind the action. This does not mean that your ethics or your honor is situational.

Let's look at stealing for example. If you were to steal a case of dynamite from a farmer down the road because you wanted that dynamite for yourself or your own personal use, that would obviously be a dishonorable act. But if you knew that this so-called farmer was actually a terrorists and was planning to use that dynamite to blow up the local school, and you went on a mission to steal the dynamite in order to stop this from happening, it would obviously be a different situation.

In the latter situation, this act would be honorable. In both cases, you stole the man's dynamite which was legally his property, so what makes one act honorable and one act dishonorable? It is the circumstances in which it occurred. It is the intention behind the action. Honor is not a set of rules carved in stone; it is concerned with your own personal code and the intentions of your heart.

95

Perfection is attained by slow degrees; she requires the hand of time.
Voltaire

I have stated many times that the ultimate objective of the warrior is the perfection of character, as Gichin Funakoshi stated in his book Karate-Do Kyohan. The perfection of your character is not a simple thing. It actually is very complex and consists of various intertwined parts which are personal for each person. Perfecting your character is not a concrete goal in which once you have done a, b, and c, you have achieved success and can then move on to a new goal.

It is a never-ending quest for excellence, and it takes time. As Voltaire stated, it is attained by slow degrees, not overnight. You must make a decision to work at perfecting your character on a daily basis. There are opportunities every day to either move forward toward your goal or to slip backward away from your ultimate objective. Many people seem to be caught in the ebb and flow of this struggle. They move one step forward and two steps back.

In order to achieve this goal, or any other goal for that matter, you cannot afford to allow the tide of life to move you back and forth. You must be focused and determined to achieve any objective, this includes perfecting your character. In fact, it is even truer when it comes to your character. Each step backward not only takes you further from the perfection of your character, but it also makes it easier to compromise the next time, which makes achieving your goal in the future even more difficult. Be disciplined and patient.

96

Victorious warriors win first and then go to war, defeated warriors go to war first then seek to win.
Sun Tzu

Preparation is vital when it comes to a physical confrontation. You can't wait until the thug is at your door to go learn some martial arts techniques, lift some weights, and do some stretching. You will never be successful if you wait to study for the test until you walk into the classroom, sit down, and receive your test. That would be ridiculous. You have to be prepared for what you may have to encounter long before you actually encounter it. You must think ahead.

This is the way of the victorious warrior. He knows that he must be prepared to meet the wolf anytime that he leaves his house, and possibly without leaving his home. He realizes that the skills which he will need to keep himself and his loved-ones safe take time to develop and perfect. They do not just magically appear like a genie from a bottle. It takes months and years of hard work to acquire the skills, techniques, and mental toughness that you will need when confronted by a skilled street fighter.

Don't do like so many others and go into battle unprepared, thinking that the adrenaline that they feel, from their anger, will pull them through to victory. This is what Sun Tzu meant by defeated warriors going to war first and then seeking to win. They enter a conflict unprepared, and then seek to win by whatever means they can. The victorious warrior on the other hand, prepares for victory long before he enters into battle. He knows when to fight, and how to fight, and therefore he ends up victorious, even without fighting.

97

Let what works well
be the test for what is right.
Bruce Lee

Don't sell out to any one style of martial art. What I mean by this is that you should not get caught up in the ongoing debate about which martial art is best, and disregard the rest as misguided simply because they are different. There is no "best" martial art or "superior" martial art. It is not going to matter in the street whether you are performing a tae kwon do kick or a karate kick. What will matter is whether or not your kick kept you safe.

This is what Bruce Lee was trying to tell us, and what was behind his martial arts as a whole. He did not believe in a specific style of martial art. Lee went on to state that you should, "Take what is useful from all styles and make it work for you." The key here is "what works for you." Everyone has specific strengths and weaknesses. Not everyone has the same body, and not every technique is appropriate for every person. Certain kicks and styles are more appropriate for some people than they are for others.

What matters is that you learn what you need to know to keep yourself and those around you safe, and once you learn the skills that you need, you keep them sharp. You may find that certain kicks are awkward for you. If so, keep practicing them, but by all means don't try to use them in a life-or death situation, at least not until you have become proficient with them. There is no "correct" form in the street. What is "correct" in the street is what brings you home alive, be it a perfectly placed karate kick or a brick.

98

Virtue, then, is a state of character concerned with choice.
Aristotle

Virtue is a good or admirable quality. It is the quality of being morally good or righteous, and it is a choice. You make the choice concerning whether or not you will foster virtuous traits in your life. As Aristotle taught, virtue is a state of character – a state of character concerned with choice, and as it is your choice, you alone have to take the responsibility of the consequences of that choice.

There will be certain consequences that come with virtuous actions, and certain consequences that follow actions which are not virtuous. The choice is yours and yours alone. The sages throughout the ages have told us that the rewards of virtue are great, yet it seems that the majority of people choose a different path. Why would they choose a different path if the rewards of virtue are so good? The answer is because they choose to take the path of least resistance.

It takes effort and relentless work to develop and live by the traits of the virtuous man. Most people are not willing to put forth the effort to live a virtuous life. Sure, they would like to have the rewards of virtue, but they consider it too much work to achieve those rewards, so they are content living a life of convenient virtue. This means that they choose to live a virtuous life as long as it is convenient for them, and set their virtue aside when it becomes inconvenient. Thus they have chosen their character.

99

When nothing can be done about the way things are, the wise stop worrying about the situation.

Lao Tzu

It seems that in today's society, many people are addicted to worry. They worry about the weather, they worry about the economy, they worry about their health, and the list goes on and on. Does their worrying accomplish anything? Well, actually it does have an effect. Everything that you do carries with it some significance. I guess the question should be, does their worrying accomplish anything constructive. In this case the answer would be, "No!"

Your thoughts have power. Worrying, like all of your thoughts, affects your mind and your body, but it does nothing to change the situation that you are worrying about in the first place. Worry is a totally useless thought process. Don't worry about things. If you can do something to help the situation, do it. If you can't do anything about the way things are, then don't waste time worrying about it.

Spend your time in ways which produce positive and useful results. If you have a problem, don't worry about it, but rather think rationally about what you can do to fix the problem. Realize that not worrying about something does not mean that you just ignore it. Take steps to protect yourself. Do what you can and then move on. The wise man will continue to monitor certain things and stay aware of the current situation, without allowing his mind to be troubled by the things which are out of his control.

100

The steadfastness of the wise is but the art of keeping their agitation locked in their hearts.
La Rochefoucauld

Everyone gets angry and disconcerted at times. This is a normal part of being human, but while certain things have a way of rubbing you the wrong way, you don't have to make that information public. La Rochefoucauld taught that the wise man will keep these things private – locked in his heart. This is where his appearance of steadfastness comes from and why people see him as a man of self-control and restraint.

He does not express his displeasure with everything that annoys him. Like anyone he can become upset, frustrated, and angry, but he has the wisdom and insight to keep his emotions private unless he has a specific reason for expressing those emotions. Everything the wise man, the warrior, does is calculated. No action is performed out of thoughtlessness. This includes making a decision concerning when and how to express his anger over specific things.

This especially includes allowing his temper or frustration to control him. He is a master of keeping his emotions in check. His agitation is kept locked in his heart, at least until he decides it is time to release it to achieve his objective if need be. No one has respect for a man who cannot control his temper or who walks around with a negative attitude concerning every little thing which has annoyed him. You must command respect, and in order to do so, you must be worthy of respect and act in a respectful manner.

101

Those skilled at making the enemy move do so by creating a situation to which he must conform.
Sun Tzu

You must become an expert in the art of winning without fighting. This may sound strange to you, but once you understand, it makes perfect sense. To illustrate I will use a scene from one of Bruce Lee's movies, *Enter the Dragon*. During a short boat ride with other fighters, Bruce Lee is accosted by another fighter, who is, of course, obnoxious and rude, and who wants to fight Lee. He pushes and pushes until Lee agrees to fight him. Lee suggests that they fight on a nearby island that can be seen from the boat.

The man agrees and Lee suggests that the two men board a small boat for a short boat ride over to the island. Again, the rude man agrees and heads toward the row boat, with Lee right behind him. As the pushy fighter makes his way into the row boat, Lee simply unties the rope which was holding the row boat to the side of the ship and lets it drift away without oars, thus defeating this enemy without fighting. The enemy lost, not because of Lee's martial arts skills, but because of his superior strategy.

This is a great example of making the enemy move by creating a situation to which he must conform. This thug would have looked like a coward had he refused to fight on the island after challenging Lee. Thus he had to agree to take the row boat over to the island and fight. Lee created a situation to which he had to conform, and the challenger did so freely. Lee made his enemy move, and at the same time defeated his enemy without fighting. This is the best and safest way to defeat an enemy. Think about this.

102

Some have been thought brave, because they were afraid to run away.
English Proverb

You can't see inside someone else's heart. Most of the time, you never really know what is going on in their mind or what their true intention is at any given moment. As this old English proverb states, many people are thought to be brave based on outward appearances rather than based on their true courage. Does it take more courage to follow your peers or to turn and go your own way? Don't get me wrong here, I am not suggesting that it is courageous to turn your back and run when you should make a stand.

What I am saying, and what this proverb implies, is that you cannot always judge whether or not someone is brave or courageous simply by observing their external actions. While it is true that many times you can detect courage by someone's actions, this does not always hold true. Sometimes we misjudge someone's intentions and character by only observing the outside and ignoring what is happening on the inside.

To really know if someone is courageous and honorable, we need to have insight into what is going on inside that person's mind. Is he acting out of a sense of courage or is he acting out of rage? Is he acting out of a sense of courage or is he too prideful to walk away? These are things to consider. We should be careful about making judgments where others are concerned because we hardly ever have all the information that we need to make a complete assessment.

103

A man has no more character than he can command in a time of crisis.
Ralph W. Sockman

Just as you can tell who your true friends are in difficult times, you can also judge someone's true character in times of crisis. It is easy to have friends when you are prosperous and times are good, but these so-called "friends" seem to disappear at the speed of light when your fortune turns on you. Your character is much the same. It is easy to talk the talk when things are going well and there is no pressure on you, but it is in times of crisis that you know your true character.

This does not mean that if you slip and falter during a crisis, that you aren't a man of integrity. Everyone makes mistakes and everyone can give in during a time of weakness, this doesn't mean that you are a man of low character. One action does not define a man, although it may in the eyes of others. Only you know who you truly are and whether or not you are a man of character and honor, but at the same time, a man of character will exhibit those traits, both on a daily basis, and in times of crisis.

In order to maintain your character during a crisis, when everyone and everything seems to be against you, you have to be prepared beforehand. This is why the warrior works to perfect his character on a daily basis. If you do not train and hone your martial arts skills before the predator attacks you, you will not be able to defend yourself. You will be unprepared. If you do not work to build your character during your daily life, you will not be strong enough to maintain that character when your back is against the wall.

104

Courage is resistance to fear, mastery of fear – not absence of fear.
Mark Twain

How many times have you heard something like, "He is really brave. He is not afraid of anything?" I know that I have heard that comment or similar ones many times. Is this real courage or simply the sign of someone with a severe lack of discretion? It is common sense to fear certain things. For example, you should have a healthy fear of jumping off the top of a 10 story building. Even though you should not allow your fears to control you, you should use common sense.

As Mark Twain explained, courage is not an absence of fear, but rather a mastery of fear. Everyone has their own fears, but the man who acts out of a sense of courage, takes control of his fear instead of allowing his fear to control his actions. He acts in spite of his fear. His fear does not dictate his actions. His actions are based on rational thought and his fear is shelved if it is contrary to what needs to be done.

This is what Mark Twain meant when he wrote that, "Courage is resistance to fear, mastery of fear – not absence of fear." The warrior must master his fear, whatever it may be, in order to act with a sense of courage. It does not matter if it is standing up to a group of thugs, or walking away from one man to accomplish his objective without a fight, both actions require courage, and both actions require the warrior to deal with specific fears. Once again, the struggle to perfect your character begins on the inside.

105

Never tolerate injustice and corruption… never be afraid to attack wrong.
Joseph Pulitzer

Never be afraid to attack wrong, or to set injustice and corruption right. This could be the motto of the warrior. It is part of the warrior's service to others to stand of up those who need his help and to never tolerate injustice or corruption when it is in his power to do something about it. This mind set is central to the warrior's code of honor, and is one of the reasons that he spends much of his time training. He must be ready to meet "wrong" head-on when he crosses paths with those who would do wrong to others.

While this is the prevailing attitude of the true warrior, he must also take into consideration that there is a correct time, correct place, and correct way to set wrongs right. Don't jump into a certain situation, with the intent to set things right, without thinking rationally about what would be appropriate. Jumping in unprepared or uninformed is acting on emotion instead of acting on rational thought. Acting on your emotions can be dangerous.

Yes, you should do what you can to set things right when you witness injustice, corruption, and wrong doing, but at the same time, you have to be smart. If you know that there is a bridge out down the road, you should certainly warn oncoming traffic. But you should do so in a safe and rational way. You could ensure that the next car would stop by standing in the middle of the road, but you could possibly be hit and die, or you could think rationally and flag that car down from a safe position. Think before you act.

106

Just as a stick must be either straight or crooked, so a man must be either just or unjust.
Zeno the Stoic

The warrior must be a just man, this goes without saying, but what is a just man? Being just means being fair and impartial, and being morally correct. It does not necessarily mean following a specific set of rules, as our legal system seems to think. Fair does not mean equal. To many people, the concept of being "fair" means everyone gets the exact same thing, whether it is punishment or a reward, according to the standards which have been agreed to or set up.

Once again, I tend to disagree with this line of thinking. Being just does not mean treating everyone exactly the same. Each situation and each person must be looked at individually to determine what is just in each specific case. This said, there is no way that a "one size fits all" model is either fair or just. This form of justice is actually injustice in many cases. A better definition of what it means to be just is that of being morally correct in every situation of your life.

Being morally correct does not mean treating everyone the same; it simply means responding to everyone and every situation in a morally just way. Each situation is different, just as each person is different, and must be addressed accordingly. This is not how most people look at justice, but as I have said before, the true warrior lives by a different code than most people. He is more concerned about truly being just, than simply appearing just in the eyes of others. Reflect on this.

107

What we do upon some great occasion will probably depend on what we already are; and what we already are will be the result of previous years of self-discipline.
Percy Bysshe Shelley

You respond to every situation from where you are at that very moment, that is all that you can do. Those people who are prepared to meet the challenges of the current situation are victorious, and those who are unprepared, many times find defeat. How you respond to an emergency situation depends on how prepared you are and who you are when that emergency situation arises. Both of those factors depend on you. You have almost total control over those two things.

How prepared you are and the kind of person you are depend on what you have done in the past to prepare yourself and to mold yourself for the present moment. If you haven't taken the time to prepare yourself, then you won't be prepared, period. Preparedness does not happen by accident; it takes months and years of self-discipline. Being a couch potato will not prepare you to be victorious on that occasion when you meet some street thug in the parking lot, set on doing you harm.

It takes years of self-discipline to be prepared to meet such a dire situation and come out victorious. That is a result of self-discipline and training, not luck. How you will respond to a life-threatening situation depends on how you have prepared to respond to that kind of situation. You can only respond as who you are now, not who you once were or who you hope to be. And who you are now depends on what you have done in the past to become the person you are today. Train hard and be prepared; your enemies are.

108

The very first step in self-restraint is the restraint of thoughts.
Gandhi

I have talked a lot about exercising self-control and self-discipline. I have also talked about the power of your thoughts. Your thoughts are not harmless bubbles which pop into your head. They contain energy and are powerful, and they do have consequences. Therefore if you are going to practice self-control, you must learn to control your thoughts first. Your thoughts are the beginning of every other action, and not controlling your thoughts will make self-control and self-discipline almost impossible.

Don't assume, as most people do, that you can think whatever you want as long as you don't act on your thoughts. This line of thinking will make attaining your goal of perfecting your character much harder to achieve. In fact, you cannot truly attain the perfection of character without restraining your thoughts and cleansing your mind. Things have to get right on the inside before they can get right on the outside. Your external actions may look right, but if your thoughts are not in line with your actions, it is only an illusion.

Work to restrain your negative thoughts and to change your thought processes and align them with who you truly are as a warrior. I say "work to restrain your thoughts" because it does take work. Restraining your thoughts does not come naturally. If all the exceptional character traits of the true warrior were easily obtained, they would not be exceptional, but rather common place. When thoughts that are contrary to the warrior lifestyle enter your mind, restrain them and replace them with noble thoughts.

109

**Understand the spirit of those with whom you deal...
the man of passion always speaks of matters far
differently from what they are...thus does everyone
babble according to his feelings or his moods,
and all, very far from the truth.**
Baltasar Gracian

You have to learn how to read people. If you simply go by what someone says, you will find that you are being misled much of the time. Most people have some agenda they wish to promote. This agenda does not necessarily have to be evil or conniving, many times it isn't, but most people have an agenda nonetheless. The wise warrior will understand this and look more at the spirit of the person he is conversing with instead of simply listening to what he is saying.

Try to discern what is behind the words. Is this person angry or upset? Is this person in a bad mood? Is this person trying to purposely deceive you? Is this person responding in a certain way because of low self-esteem or in an attempt to save face? There could be many reasons for his behavior. Learn how to read people and how to see past the façade that they maintain. Marcus Aurelius said to "look within things," and that is exactly what the warrior should do, look past the words and look within the person.

Realize, as Baltasar Gracian said, that almost everyone speaks according to his feelings and moods, and many times what they say is far from being the truth. You have to work to get to the truth most of the time. People hide the truth for different reasons, but just know that they will and do hide the truth. Listen to the true meaning behind the words instead of the words themselves.

110

A man's action is only a picture book of his creed.
Emerson

How do you know what someone truly believes? Look at their actions. You have heard the old saying that actions speak louder than words, this is absolutely true. Your actions do speak louder than your words and you can bet that people will pay more attention to what you do than to what you say. If your actions and your words are not in sync this will be apparent to the casual observer and they will likely challenge you on this, as they should, especially where the warrior is concerned.

The warrior's actions and his words should be consistent with each other. He should say what he means and mean what he says. His creed or code should shine through in his daily actions. There should not be any discrepancy between the two. Sincerity is an important part of the warrior lifestyle. You are not acting in a certain manner just to impress those around you; your code of ethics has to be real and a part of who you truly are as a warrior.

Your actions portray who you really are and they should coincide with the standards that you profess as a warrior. Saying one thing and doing another is the behavior of a hypocrite, not a man of honor. This is not how you want people to see you as a warrior. No one respects someone who is insincere and contrived. Make the traits of the warrior lifestyle a part of who you truly are and live them. Don't just give them lip service. Take your character seriously and mold it according to the standards of the warrior.

111

We know too much and are convinced of too little.
T. S. Eliot

If you are truly convinced of something, you will act on it. The sages throughout the ages taught that to know is to act. If you don't use what you have learned, what good is it? Today we read many things and have access vast amounts of information, but are we really convinced that what we know is true? Most people must not be convinced because they are not really acting on the knowledge which they have acquired. If you really know something and are convinced it is true, you will use that knowledge.

For example, you have the knowledge that if some thug sticks a six inch blade into your body, it is going to do some severe damage to you, and could possibly kill you. Knowing this, you take steps to make sure that this does not happen. You are convinced that this is true and therefore you act on this information by staying clear of thugs with knives. But what about other things such as eating junk food. Are you really convinced that junk food will damage your health and make it harder to achieve your goals?

There is a Hadith that states, "The truly learned are those who apply what they know." If you are not truly convinced that something is true, you will not act on it; if on the other hand, you are truly convinced that something is true, you will act on it. It seems that many people amass considerable knowledge, but are convinced of very little. Are you convinced that the path of the warrior is the right path for you? If so, are you acting on that conviction and making the traits of the warrior lifestyle part of your daily life?

112

When walking, walk.
When eating, eat.
Zen Maxim

Awareness is not just for the streets and dark alleyways. You should be engaged no matter what you are doing. Focus on the matter at hand, whatever that may be. While multi-tasking may be the way of the world right now, and almost everyone does it at some time, you should practice focusing on one thing at a time. This is the meaning behind this Zen maxim. Whatever you are doing, focus all your attention on that one thing and then move on to the next.

This means when you are engaged in a martial arts workout, you should concentrate on your workout, not your bills, your problems, or what you are going to do next. Simply focus on your workout until you are finished working out. Then you can decide what to focus on next. If you will approach your workouts with this mental clarity, you will find that your skills will improve much faster and that you will start to see greater gains in both flexibility and strength.

As I have said before, there is power in your thoughts. When you focus your thoughts on the task at hand, you are integrating your energy with whatever it is that you are doing. This can be compared to being in "the zone." You are focused and mentally engaged in the present moment. This should be how the warrior approaches every task that he attempts – with one pointed focus. Like all the other parts of the warrior lifestyle, this too requires practice to perfect, but it is attainable. Be in the zone; focus on the Now.

113

Do every act of your life as if it were your last.
Marcus Aurelius

Everything that you do should be done to the highest standards. This is especially true for the warrior whose goal it is to be a man of excellence. Shortcuts are very tempting, particularly when we are engaged in a mundane or trivial task, but the warrior should not be satisfied with mediocrity. He aspires to excellence. Whether you are building a new room on your house, or weeding your garden, put your best effort into the task. This is a good way to practice self-discipline.

Self-discipline is a major part of the warrior lifestyle. Without it, not much would be accomplished because it requires a lot of self-discipline to work on your character, to study, to workout, or to lift weights, when you simply feel like sitting in your recliner and watching television. You could say that the cornerstone of the warrior lifestyle is self-discipline; it is that important. Putting your heart and soul into every action, as if it were your last, definitely takes a lot of self-discipline.

Why should you do every act as if it were your last? The simple answer is because the warrior is a man of excellence, and as a man of excellence you should strive to do whatever you do to the best of your ability. If you need more reason to pursue excellence, the answer is that you are not really, truly alive when you don't. To be truly alive, you can't walk through life on autopilot. You have to be focused and aware. You have to completely live every moment of your life to the best of your ability.

114

Even Time, the father of all, cannot undo what has been done, whether right or wrong.
Pindar

What is done, is done. There are no do-over's; there are no "King's aces." Once you take action, that action, whether right or wrong, cannot be undone. This is something that the warrior should consider. For this reason, you should consider every action carefully before you make your move. Think about the possible consequences of every action *before* you act. Look at the different options, and choose wisely. Rash action many times leads to trouble and heartache.

This same principle applies to your speech as well as your actions. Once a word is spoken, it can never be taken back. Many hurtful things have been said, out of anger and frustration, which set a chain of events in motion which can never be undone. Not only will the wise warrior think before he takes action, but he will also think before he speaks. Both misguided actions and thoughtless words can damage you in ways which you could never imagine.

So what do you do if you find that this advice comes too late, and you have already done or said something you wish you could retract? The answer is the same for everyone. All you can do is do your best at this present moment. If you have made mistakes, there is nothing you can do to change history. What you can do is take steps to set things right, and make a firm decision to start living as you should. The past cannot be changed; we can only act in the present moment. Make the present moment right.

115

Most of the time we are only partially alive.
Marcel Proust

Too many people today live their lives on auto-pilot. They function and live their lives day by day, week by week, month by month, without really being alive. Sure they are breathing and they have blood pumping through their veins, but they are a bit like zombies – the living dead. This is what Marcel Proust called being only "partially alive." A person fitting this characterization is alive, but is not really living his life. He is only going through the motions.

Life is way too short for us to simply walk through it on auto-pilot, not really enjoying it, but merely staying alive and going through the same old, same old each day. People who "live" this way will find that they will have many regrets when they reach old age, and they will also find that they will reach old age much faster than they ever thought. Life is short, even for those who live every day to the fullest. Don't take it for granted, moping through each day with no enthusiasm.

The warrior lifestyle leads to a life that is fully lived. Warriors refuse to walk around only partially alive. They strive for excellence and make a point to live their lives to the fullest. You do this by being in the moment, being aware of the significance of each and every minute. This is what is meant by the Zen maxim which states, "When walking, walk. When eating, eat." Be present in this moment. Live 60 seconds, every minute. Don't waste the time you have been given. Find that spark that you need to be fully alive. Live your life.

116

Old and young,
we are all on our last cruise.
Robert Louis Stevenson

The average person looks at life differently than the warrior. Joe Blow looks at life in the terms of "what is in it for me." He thinks to himself, "Life is short, so I should get mine. I'm not worried about anyone else." To him to concept of sacrificing his time or comfort to live the lifestyle of the warrior is preposterous. He would never consider sacrificing his comfort or his profits for the sake of honor or integrity. If he can get away doing something dubious, he is satisfied, as long as it serves his needs.

This type of person is short-sighted. He does not understand that he has only one chance to become a man of character, and that when he comes to the end of his life's journey, he will have many regrets because of the way that he has lived his life. The warrior also knows that life is short, but instead of serving his greed, he makes a decision to be a man of excellence. He chooses to live a life filled with honor, integrity and service to others. He refuses to seek personal fulfillment at the expense of others.

Everyone is on their last cruise, and it is up to each individual to choose his own itinerary. You decide which direction you will take and you chart your own course. You choose the type ship that you will board and the people who will accompany you on your trip. It is up to you what places you will visit and how you will conduct yourself throughout your cruise. Will you step on others at every dock or will you leave a lasting legacy of honor from port to port? This is your final cruise – travel wisely.

117

Until you have rectified yourself, you cannot rectify others.
Chinese Proverb

You must make sure that you are living your life right before you even think about telling someone else how to live their life. Too many people have this backwards. They want to give everyone else advice on living, but they don't want to take the time and effort to make sure their own life is the way it should be. It seems that they thrive on minding other people's business, but find self-improvement a boring proposition. Are these people really interested in helping others, or do they just like being entertained.

The warrior is a master of focusing on his own self-improvement, while at the same time being there for his friends and family when they need his advice or help. He is too busy trying to perfect his own character, improving his martial arts skills, and improving his intellect, to be a busybody. At the same time, he is willing to set his own wants aside to help those in need, but he is careful about how he goes about this, knowing that he cannot rectify others without first making sure that he is who he should be.

The word "rectify" means to correct something or to purify something. In the same way you would not go to someone who cannot balance their own checkbook for financial advice, you should not offer to correct someone else's problems if you cannot manage your own affairs. First, make your own life right, and then seek to help others correct their shortcomings. The warrior should seek to help others, especially those close to him, but no one should try to correct the faults of others before they have addressed their own faults.

118

Surprise defeats strength and speed.
Glenn Morris

An enemy surprised is half defeated. This is a common statement seen in many martial arts books. I don't care who you are or how advanced your martial arts skills may be, there are people out there who are bigger, tougher and more talented. They will be stronger and faster. Even if you are the best there is today, that will change next year or in the next ten years. Some day you will find that you are no longer the best of the best (if you ever were).

When that day comes, you will have to find ways to compensate for the fact that there are many bad guys out there who you cannot stand up to toe-to-toe in a physical confrontation. One of the ways to counteract the current of the river which keeps pulling you downstream is to develop superior strategy. Using the element of surprise is one of the strategic moves that can give you the edge that you need. As the Ninja Master, Glen Morris, states, surprise defeats strength and speed.

This is a very good thing for the aging warrior because as we age, our strength and speed regress. The element of surprise makes the battle ground even again, or even tilts the odds in your favor. This is even more true if you are still at the peak of your skills as a martial artist. If you are still among the best, think how much harder you will be to defeat if you integrate the element of surprise into your arsenal. Don't rely solely on your techniques, your speed, or your strength, throw in the element of surprise and make all the rest more devastating.

119

All you learn, and all you can read, will be of little use, if you do not think and reason upon it yourself.
Lord Chesterfield

The true gentleman warriors of old made learning and studying part of their lifestyle, and so should you. Study different subjects from history to great wisdom literature, and from martial arts to gardening. The range of subjects is only limited by your interests and your imagination. You should study and be well balanced, but make sure that when you read and study, you make good use of your time. Learning is not about rote memorization; it is about a complete understanding of your subject.

It is pretty much a waste of time to read something when your mind is somewhere else. Remember the Zen maxim, "When eating, eat. When walking, walk." Well I might add, when studying, study. Engage your mind fully in what you are reading. Reason upon it, as Lord Chesterfield urged his son to do. Debate what you have learned in your mind. Think on it until you have come to understand it fully. Don't merely breeze through it, but savor it completely.

Don't multi-task when you are reading or studying. Turn off the television and focus on the information at hand. This is using your time wisely. If you are not truly engaging your mind during your reading time, you will not gain any long-term value from what you have read. Real knowledge involves using what you have learned. How can you use what you have "learned" if you really don't understand what you have "learned?"

120

As a human being one should train one's mind and one's ability to the fullest.
Miyamoto Musashi

If you are going to do something, do it right. This is essentially what Miyamoto Musashi, the great Japanese swordsman, was trying to tell us. Don't settle for mediocrity. Develop your mind and your body to the best of your ability. I might add to Musashi's admonition, to also develop your spirit to the best of your ability. The warrior, as I have said many times, is a man of excellence. Whatever he does, he does 100%, whether it is gardening or honing his martial arts skills.

Musashi only touched on two areas in this quote – your mind and your skills. Many martial artists spend much more time working on their martial arts skills than their minds, but both are important. You should strive for balance. No matter what you do, you can't allow yourself to become so focused on that one thing, that you become unbalanced. It doesn't matter what that passion may be. It could be martial arts or it could be golf. Whatever your passion is, it is important that you maintain balance in your life.

Maintaining balance means that you exercise enough discipline to not allow any one thing to manipulate all of your time. The warrior is a man of balance. He must schedule his time in order to fit in all the things which are important to develop on his path to warriorship. He has to develop his mind, his body and his spirit. Too much time spent on any one area will lead to an imbalance or weakness in one of the other areas. Train your mind, body and spirit to the fullest, but make sure to maintain a sense of balance.

121

Never trust your tongue
when your heart is bitter.
Samuel J. Hurwitt

When you are angry, and especially when you are very angry, it is best to remain silent. You will almost certainly end up saying things that you will later regret, if you indulge yourself and allow yourself to rant and rave when you are in the grasp of an angry or hurt heart. When someone is in the grasp of anger, he speaks from his emotions rather than from rational thought. Therefore he allows his emotions to temporarily take over, until the anger has subsided.

Letting your emotions take charge of your decisions, whether it is your actions or your speech, is always a dangerous proposition. At such times, you are not fully rational. You lash out and say things which you don't mean. Oh maybe you mean them at that point in time, but your feelings quickly change when you have calmed down and are back to thinking rationally. But then it is too late. The cat has already been let out of the bag, and now you have the monumental task of trying to control that wild cat that you let loose.

It is better by far, to recognize when anger has flared up inside you, and make a conscious decision to remain silent, at least until a later time. This is not easy to do, but it can be done, and it will save you a lot of stress and hassles if you will simply make firm decision to control your tongue. Look at anger as a trap, set to trip you up and knock you down. Be smart enough to recognize the traps which are set by your enemies and avoid them. Learn to control your tongue, especially when you are angry.

122

Don't tell your secret even to a fence.
Irish Proverb

I cannot overstate the need to guard your private matters with silence. Avoid sharing all of your private information with other people. There are many reasons why you should safeguard personal information, but the main reason is that people who don't are continually inviting a variety of problems. I could give you hundreds of examples of people who have caused problems for themselves that would not have existed had they heeded this simple warning.

The desire to gossip and chat about private matters, is tempting to many. Some people seem to thrive on gossip. When someone starts sharing juicy secrets, it is as if you just brought in a plate with a steaming hot, juicy steak, and placed it in front of them. They love it and they can't wait to share it with others. This is the main reason that you should not share your secrets with other people. If you could not resist the urge to talk about that juicy secret, how do you expect someone else to resist the urge to share it?

After all, you shared your secret with them, and you actually had something to lose by sharing that information, not them. You could not resist talking about it, even though it might cost you. Why would you expect them not to talk about it when there is no risk to them at all in sharing your private information? That is pure foolishness. If you have a secret, and we all do, keep it to yourself! Find something else to chat about, or better yet spend your time in a productive way, instead of chit-chatting about meaningless things.

123

Feel the warrior within you.
Loren W. Christensen

I have covered a lot of character traits, details, and ideals which apply to the true warrior in the *Warrior Wisdom* series, but none of the things which I have covered will make any real difference to you if you don't internalize them. You must take the warrior lifestyle seriously for it to affect your life. Don't simply dabble with it, like a child who sticks his toe in the pool, but is afraid to just jump in and enjoy the water. Immerse yourself completely in it and allow it transform your life.

You must feel the warrior within you, as Loren Christensen says. This means that you have to know, deep inside, that you are a true warrior, no matter what anyone else says or thinks. Only you know who you truly are. You must feel the warrior spirit inside. Know that you live by your code of honor and that you stand by your principles and standards, against the greatest foe and in the most difficult times. Take the warrior lifestyle seriously in spite of what others may say about you or your goals.

Others may not understand you, and that does not matter. What does matter is that you have made a firm decision to walk the path of the warrior. No one can stop you from working to perfect your character, and striving for excellence in all the other aspects of the warrior lifestyle. It is you, and you alone, who has to make the decision that you will live the life of the warrior. You must build your own fire, and then you have to keep it fueled. You have to feel the warrior within you, and then keep him strong.

124

The wise conquer by strength, rather than anger.
Nagarjuna

Many guys out there believe that when they get angry they are unstoppable. They feel that rush of adrenaline, and in their mind it feels like they have just slipped into Superman's tights, complete with cape and super powers. Although that boost of adrenaline can put you into a different state of mind, it is not always a positive thing, especially if you allow your anger to control your actions. It is wiser by far to use your strength, your skills, and your mind, to defeat your opponent, than hope to achieve victory with your anger.

There is a Japanese proverb that states that, "A quick temper does not bring success." This is wisdom that is shared throughout the world, and down through the ages. All of the sages have warned against allowing your anger to control your actions. But, as with many wise teachings, this is easier said than done, especially when someone has blatantly wronged you. Controlling your anger takes conscious effort, and even those who have mastered this skill, still struggle with it on occasion.

There are many anger management techniques out there that you can experiment with, and if this area is a problem for you, I recommend that you try them out. Breath work is one which many warriors and police offers use to both control their anger and help them stay calm under stressful situations. The one thing that you must do when you feel your anger rising to a "dangerous" level, is to be aware of what is happening and strive to think rationally. Once anger has taken over, rational thought has taken a back seat.

125

Living well is the best revenge.
George Herbert

To many warriors, one of their most intricate struggles deals with the act of revenge. It requires great self-discipline to allow someone, who has completely wronged you, to walk away with no consequences for his actions. This can be especially trying for the warrior since he has the skills and knowledge to make the wrongdoer pay, and pay severely for his transgression. It seems to be human nature to want someone who has greatly hurt you, to pay for what they have done, to also feel pain, for what they did to you.

The best tome that I have read concerning the subject of revenge came from a chapter in the book, *Living the Martial Way*, by Forrest Morgan. He covers the difference in revenge and in avenging a wrong in specific detail that is geared towards the warrior, as is his whole book. If you haven't read that book, you should get a copy and read it. All of the sages taught us that we should not take revenge on those who wrong us. Although we know this inside, it is still something that many of us struggle with throughout our lives.

George Herbert stated that living well is the best revenge, but it does not seem like it at the time your emotions are still running wild with anger over what has happened. It takes time to recover from certain things. It does not happen overnight. One thing to keep in mind, if you are fighting an internal battle with feelings of revenge, is to not act rashly. Give yourself time and distance yourself from the incident in order to be able to think rationally. To do otherwise is the same as letting your emotions cloud your mind.

126

One has to face fear
or forever run from it.
Hawk

Your fear will haunt you until you find the courage to face it. Most of the time, when you finally find the courage to face the thing that you fear, you find that it was not as bad as you thought it was. Once you meet your fear head on, the thing that you feared loses its power over you. It no longer haunts your mind or causes you to lose sleep. Your imagination and mental visions, concerning how bad that thing that you fear is going to be, makes your fear appear worse than it is in reality.

One way to approach your fear, is to ask yourself, "What is the worst thing that can happen?" For example, you may fear having to spar with a certain fighter in your martial arts class. Maybe he is a foot taller than you, his skills are excellent, and on top of that, he is ripped from spending many additional hours in the weight room. Every time your class gets ready to spar, your heart is pounding with the fear that you will get picked to match skills with this natural "destroyer."

Ask yourself, "What is the worst thing that could happen if I get drawn to fight this guy?" In reality, the worst thing that could happen is that you get pounded, but this is not a street fight. You will both be wearing protective gear. It could be a bit embarrassing, but you will live through it, and maybe you will learn some things and gain some confidence. This is not that bad. See what I mean? Facing your fears is something that requires rational thought. Don't let your imagination make the wolf bigger than he really is.

127

The future is purchased by the present.
French Proverb

Your future depends on the decisions that you make today. The decisions that you make today will have consequences or results that you will see tomorrow, next week, next month, next year, and maybe for the rest of your life. Short-sighted people do not seem to realize this. Instead of working hard and preparing for tomorrow, they avoid discipline and merely live for the moment. It appears that this person enjoys a better life. He is always having fun. He is always up for a party.

In reality, he is not enjoying a better life. He is simply living a life void of discipline, goals and purpose. He is short-sighted and unwise. Soon his lack of discipline and preparation will catch up with him and he will be heart-sick, especially when he observes the life of his counterpart who lived with direction and discipline. The man, who elects to live life with discipline, still enjoys his life, but he has the wisdom to prepare for the future at the same time.

He knows that the future is not that far away, and that he must prepare today if he wants his future to be comfortable. There is a Norse saying that states that you must kill the elk when you are young, if you wish to lie on the skin in old age. The warrior knows that he must prepare for the future today. You prepare for tomorrow's violent encounter, during today's training. Wasting time in the present is stealing from the future. Study, train, meditate, and prepare today for a quality future tomorrow.

128

Never underestimate an adversary.
Kazumi Tabata

There is never anything positive to be gained by underestimating your enemy, no matter how insignificant you may consider him. The only thing that underestimating your enemy can possibly do is aid your enemy in his quest to hurt you. It does nothing at all for you, at least nothing positive. Like everything that you do, it does have an effect on you though; the only thing is that effect that will be purely negative. Why in the world would you want to do something to help your enemy and hurt yourself?

Underestimating your enemy will have several consequences. First, as I already stated, it will give your enemy a bit of a break. When you underestimate someone, you make it possible for them to use the element of surprise against you because you are not expecting them to present a challenge. In reality, you don't know what he has in mind. It is folly to discount the possible adversity that he could cause you. Not only are you aiding your enemy when you underestimate him, but you are undermining your own preparedness.

When you underestimate your enemy, you are less likely to seriously prepare for an attack by him. This is only common sense. Why would you prepare to defend yourself against someone who you feel is not a serious threat? Underestimating your enemy weakens your motivation to stay ready to meet this adversary, again enabling him to use the element of surprise to his advantage. Always take every enemy seriously. Arrange things so your enemies can't hurt you, and consider each and every one of them a danger.

129

Warriorhood is action, not good intentions.
Martina Sprague

If you have read either of my first two books in the *Warrior Wisdom* series, you already know that I consider a person's intentions to be key. It is someone's intentions, the purpose behind their actions, which determine the character and honor of their actions. A good act can be tarnished by dishonorable intentions. It is the intention behind the action, and the circumstances that surround the action, which make any action either honorable or dishonorable.

At first glance, this quote by Martina Sprague seems to discount good intentions, but that is not what she is saying. What this quote means is that it takes more than good intentions; it takes both good intentions and action. Honorable thoughts or wishes alone are not enough. You must follow through. You must act. The warrior can't live in a fantasy world, where he has honorable thoughts and good intentions, but never acts on them. Dreaming is not walking the path of the warrior.

You must take those honorable thoughts and good intentions and turn them into tangible actions. In her same commentary, *Are Warriors Born or Made*, Martina Sprague also states, "A warrior is a different breed because he has conviction..." You will never turn your good intentions into action without conviction. Good intentions without conviction only lead to daydreaming, not action. While good intentions are important, in fact they are vital, they are useless if you don't act on them. Think about this.

130

Man lives freely
only by his readiness to die.
Gandhi

This is yet another concept that has been taught universally by the sages throughout the ages, and it was also a very important concept for the Samurai. *The Code of the Samurai* states, "Keep your death in mind and you will be careful and discreet with the things that you say." It also states that the Samurai should constantly keep in mind that he must die. This was not a morbid practice, but rather one which helped to keep the Samurai focused on what was important in his life.

It also kept the Samurai focused on the importance of keeping his affairs in order. He never knew when he might be killed in battle or commanded to commit seppuku, ritual suicide. Though the practice of contemplating your death and the shortness of life is an ancient practice, we can still use it today to help remind ourselves of the value of life and of why we should do our best to live right, now. Tomorrow may be too late to set things right. Now is the time to live your life.

Cicero taught that, "No man can be ignorant that he must die, nor be sure that he may not this very day." Keep this thought in mind. You don't know how much time you have to spend on this earth. You may live to be an old man or you may die in a car crash tomorrow. For this reason, it is folly for you to procrastinate. Live your life with character, honor and integrity, and live it now. Keep your affairs in order. Start today, this minute. There is no tomorrow, only the present – use it wisely.

131

I do what is mine to do;
the rest does not disturb me.
Marcus Aurelius

You only have control over one thing – yourself. You control your thoughts, your attitude, and your actions, and this is exactly where your focus should be. Do the best that you can where these things are involved and don't be disturbed by the actions, attitudes, or behavior of others. You are not responsible for what other people do; you are only responsible for what you do. Too many people want to take ownership for the acts of others, but each person is ultimately responsible for his own actions.

Do your best to be the best person that you can be and let the chips fall where they may. Once you have done your duty to the best of your ability, don't be upset if the outcome does not come out exactly as you had hoped. Simply know in your heart that you did the best that you could, given the circumstances. You acted in the moment to the best of your ability and made the best decisions that you could. What more is there?

This is the way of the warrior. If a man does what is his to do, and does it to the best of his capability, he has fulfilled his duty. Moment by moment, day by day, this is all that any man can do. Being upset or stressed out about things over which you have no control is a waste of time. Only think about such things when you can do something to change the situation. If the situation cannot be changed, what good does it do to ponder it? Be rational and concentrate on what you can do – then do it.

132

Control your mind and remain undisturbed. That is the secret of Perfect Peace.
Sai Baba

The man who really understands things at the deepest level will remain rational and undisturbed no matter what set of circumstances he happens to find himself in. He understands that it does no good to become stressed and panic, in fact, he knows that by allowing his mind to become stressed he is defeating himself within his core. You have to be able to control your mind and think rationally during times of duress; you cannot panic or let your fears take over.

This is easy for me to say while I am sitting behind a desk and writing in the comfort and safety of my own home, but how do you control your mind and remain calm and collected when you are confronted by a knife wielding thug in a parking lot? The answer is that you have to practice controlling your mind and emotions, *before* that situation ever arises. You must put yourself into these kinds of stressful situations during your normal practice sessions.

Realistic practice scenarios prepare your mind and body to deal with that rush of adrenaline that you will experience if you ever find yourself in such a situation. Dealing with these emergency situations is just like dealing with any other situation, the more experience you have, the better equipped you are to deal with the problem. This principle applies to everything in life. You become better at things as you do them, whether it is playing the piano or dealing with a violent encounter.

133

Victory is not gained through idleness
German Proverb

Oh, the comforts of home! Today, the majority of people, especially in this country have a pretty comfortable home life. Comfortable beds, nice, plush furniture to sit on, recliners, cable television, computers, stereos, the list could go on and on. There are so many things that tempt us to sit idly by and entertain our minds instead of making the effort to get up and exercise our bodies. It takes very little effort to surf the web, where it takes some discipline to get up and work on your martial arts.

You can waste hours before you know it surfing the web or sitting in front of a television set, but as this German proverb states, that is not going to help you when you are confronted by a violent thug the next time you are away from home. It is also not going to make you any younger, healthy, or stronger. Although there is a time for relaxing in front of the television and a time for surfing the net to increase your knowledge, you have to make sure that you maintain a balance between activity and inactivity.

Balance is the key. You have to balance your workouts, your martial arts training, meditation, stretching, and strength training, with relaxing, reading, and studying. Too much of anything is not good, whether it is working out or sleeping. The lifestyle of the warrior is one of balancing every part of your life – spiritually, mentally, physically, and emotionally. If any of these areas falls out of balance, all the other areas suffer as well, and complete idleness will throw them all out of balance. Employ discipline to achieve balance.

134

One who is a samurai should continually read the ancient records so that he may strengthen his character.
Code of the Samurai

The struggle to build and strengthen your character is a life-long struggle and you have to stay focused in order to be successful in the long run. One of the tools that you have at your disposal, especially today, is all of the great literature in print and on the internet. The Samurai spent time each day reading the "ancient records" and so should you. There were many writings that the Samurai studied including the teachings of Confucius and Buddha.

Today you have a multitude of wisdom writings that can help you on your path towards warriorhood. Not only can you still read the teachings of Confucius and Buddha, but you also have many more books, both ancient and modern, too many to be mentioned in this short commentary. Books such as the *Warrior Wisdom* Series, *Wisdom of the Elders*, *Modern Bushido*, and *The Secrets of Worldly Wisdom* are a good place to start. The amount of wisdom available to you today is staggering.

It is very important to continually read and study good wisdom literature in order to keep your mind focused on how you should live your life. With our hectic lifestyles today, it is easy to allow the things which we have learned to slide into the background and be forgotten if we do not keep them fresh in our mind. Develop a habit of reading something motivational and wisdom based, on a daily basis. Strengthen your character with the teachings of the elders.

135

An angry warrior is never a conscious warrior.
Scott Shaw

A conscious warrior is one who is keenly aware of his surroundings, and whose actions are intentional, considered, and deliberate. He acts with critical awareness and rational thought. If you allow your anger to control your actions, you cannot be a conscious warrior. It is just not possible. Anger will skew your thought process and your actions will no longer be considered and deliberate.

In order to be a conscious warrior, which is exactly what you should be, you have to learn to control your anger. Don't let your anger get the best of you. If you find that you have become very angry, don't act until you have your anger under control. This means that you have to think rationally. When you feel the heat of anger raging inside, shift gears and let your rational mind take over. This can be hard to do; it does take self-discipline and practice, but it can and must be done.

Your actions must be deliberate, not impulsive. Acting on impulse or a sudden urge, can get you into big trouble. This is why so many fighters and thugs in "the know," try to anger their opponents. An angry opponent is an opponent on his way to defeat. Instead of acting on impulse, stay calm and intentional. Let your rational mind, which sees through the feeble attempts of your enemy to anger you, control your actions. Mind games are like a chess match, always think before you make your move.

136

An ancient dojo was a sacred place, now it is a commercial place.
Kensho Furuya

Martial arts have changed immensely over the years. Now, instead of the dojo being a place where you find men who are training to fight and becoming men of honor, you are more likely to find a group of kids being entertained. So many dojos today have morphed into after-school programs. There is nothing wrong with children learning good character traits and participating in martial arts training. I trained my own sons in martial arts at an early age.

But, if you take a close look at many of these dojos, they are merely commercial belt factories. They do not emphasize good character traits and real self-defense skills. It is becoming increasingly harder to find a dojo that resembles the dojos of old which were considered sacred, and which took the martial arts seriously. This means that it is much harder for the true warrior to find real-life, useful training, training which he can actually use to save his life or the lives of those around him.

It is much more common to find instruction on how to win trophies, score points, or kiai loud enough to impress a group of judges, none of which makes you any safer on the street. While there is nothing wrong with martial arts competitions, this is not the real reason that the true warrior trains. He trains in order to be prepared for that unlikely encounter for which his life or the lives of his loved ones will be in danger, and when that day comes, points and trophies won't matter. All that will matter is surviving.

137

It does no good to be right yet dead.
Lawrence A. Kane

It seems that the majority of people prefer to be right, or at least prefer to think that they have proven their point, rather than to achieve their ultimate objective. Many lose sight of their overall objective when they find themselves in a conflict. They will go to the mat to "prove" their point. It doesn't matter that "proving" their point may cost them their goal. It is akin to winning the battle, but losing the war. They want to win their "battle" at all cost.

This is backwards thinking, especially for the warrior. As Lawrence Kane states in his book, *The Way of Kata*, "It does no good to be right yet dead." Instead of trying to prove that you are right, or fighting a battle because you are in the right, think of your ultimate objective. Is your ultimate objective to put the other person in his place and show him your righteous anger, or is your goal to achieve a larger victory? You have to be smart and use some strategy.

You have to think ahead, as in a chess match. Sometimes in a chess match you must sacrifice your queen in order to win. Don't be hardheaded. Be willing to sacrifice a battle in order to win the war. There is a time and a place to make your ultimate move that will put your enemy in checkmate, but you have to be smart and think ahead. Sure, you may be in the right to walk up and tell four gang members, who are polishing their guns, while sitting on your car to beat it, but would that be the smartest strategy in that situation?

138

One should constantly be in a state of preparedness.
Hironori Otsuka

It does no good to train and be skilled in your martial art if at the vital moment, that time that you find yourself in harm's way, you are unprepared. You can be prepared 99% of the time, but if your trouble comes during that small window of time that you have let your guard down, it will not matter how prepared you were the rest of the time. If you have been prepared to meet the wolf every day of the month, and decide to take a day off, and that day is the day that the wolf crosses your path, you are in trouble.

You have to be ready for trouble when trouble comes, and since you can't tell the future, you don't know when that will occur. For this reason you must maintain a constant state of preparedness. You must be ready to meet dangerous conflicts at all times. All the target practice in the world will not help you if, at the moment of truth, your gun is sitting at home in your gun cabinet. In the same way, all of your martial arts training will do you no good if you find yourself unprepared at your time of need.

Now, I'm not talking about living in a constant state of paranoia. That would not be a healthy or enjoyable way to live your life. What I am talking about is being in a state of awareness. Be aware of what is happening around you, and be ready to deal with whatever may come your way. If you decide to go out drinking, and get totally wasted one night, you are not going to be fully aware or prepared should trouble arise. This would be unwise, and is a good example of letting your guard down. Be prepared for the unexpected.

139

In inner quiet lies the salvation of the spirit.
Baltasar Gracian

Much of the training of the warrior is concerned with doing damage to the human body. That is the essence of martial arts training. The warrior spends time learning how to destroy or disable the human anatomy. He spends hours visualizing how he would respond to certain threats, how he would break this joint or break that bone. The true warrior will even spend time visualizing having to take the life of another human being if he is ever caught in that unfortunate situation.

These can be some pretty violent visualizations, and some violent techniques that the warrior learns. He has knowledge concerning things that never cross most people's minds except while watching some Hollywood movie. At the same time, the warrior has to be at peace and maintain a peaceful, loving spirit. This seems like an oxymoron. How can a person constantly train for violent situations, think about violent confrontations, and still be a peaceful person who cares for his fellow man? The answer lies in meditation.

You should learn the art of inner silence. According to Baltasar Gracian in his great book, *The Art of Worldly Wisdom*, the salvation of the spirit lies in inner quiet. Inner quiet is another term for peace, and a peaceful spirit comes through meditation. Learn to control your thoughts. Attitude control is another important technique for the warrior to master. Realize that you are learning these violent techniques to serve and protect, not for dishonorable purposes. When you know inside that your training is for the good of others, it is easy to maintain a calm spirit.

140

Good means not merely not to do wrong, but rather not to desire to do wrong.
Democritus

You can't always judge someone's character by watching what they don't do. Aristotle taught that it is much better to judge someone by what they do, not what they refrain from doing. Many people refrain from doing certain things, not because they are outstanding people of good character, but because they are afraid of the consequences of certain actions. Does this make them good people or does this make them intelligent enough not to go to jail?

Being a man of character, honor and integrity means much more than not doing things which are dishonorable and unvirtuous. Character comes from the inside; it is part of who you are deep in your spirit. The true man of character does not merely refrain from doing wrong, but rather has the strong desire to do right. Character and honor is a state of mind that shows through in his actions. If the desire to do wrong does emerge in his mind, he takes control of that thought and corrects it mentally.

As Democritus points out, being a truly good man requires both right actions and right thinking. Your thoughts and desires are just as important as your actions when it comes to true honor. Intentions play a huge role in the life of the warrior. Right actions without right intentions are not honorable, no matter how they may look to the eyes of the unknowing public. This is why so much of the time, only the person himself knows whether or not he is acting from a place of true honor.

141

You must be the change you wish to see in the world.
Gandhi

Every year we inevitably see examples on the news of people's lack of empathy for their fellow human beings. News shows will feature footage of someone being beaten, robbed, or hurt and in need of help, while people callously look on without offering to help the victim. People are horrified as they witness these scenes on television, but at the same time, the people that they are watching on the news are normal, ordinary people. They aren't necessarily evil people. They just do not want to get involved.

This is not the way of the warrior. The warrior knows that it is his duty to help his fellow human beings when it is in his power to do so. He could never witness someone being beaten, robbed, raped, or otherwise victimized and simply pass by as if he didn't notice. His code of honor and his conscience would never permit him to turn a blind eye. It is absolutely unthinkable for him to be that heartless and cowardly. Warriors are the sheepdogs, the watchmen if you will for those in need.

If those examples, which reporters love to highlight throughout the year, turn your stomach, don't wait for other people to act. Know that you have a duty. You, as a true warrior, have to be the change that you would like to see in those around you. You must be the man of excellence, even if no one else notices or cares. You aren't living the warrior lifestyle to impress others, but rather you are living it because it is the way life should be lived – with honor, integrity and character. Be the change – be a true warrior.

142

Obsessed is a word the lazy use to describe the dedicated.
Mike Reeves

Dedication – this is a word that is absent from the vocabulary of many people in the world today. People seem to want instant gratification in all things. From fast foods to music downloads, our culture is used to getting things fast, and when things don't happen as soon as people would like, they become frustrated and move on to something else. Dedication and hard work is a subject that seems to be lost on the younger generation; they are not real keen on working hard and long to achieve their objectives.

When they see someone who does put in long hours of hard work to achieve something, whether it is in sports, in their studies, martial arts, or whatever, they think that person is "obsessed" with their passion. They do not seem to understand that you have to work hard to achieve worthwhile goals. Working out for years to earn your black belt seems insane to many people. After all, who wants to "waste" that much time? What they don't understand is that anything easily obtained is not highly valued by most people.

Things worthwhile require dedication and hard work to obtain, whether it is a black belt or a college degree. Now you might argue that you can "get" both of these without that much hard work; there are ways around all those hours of work. And this is true. You could just spend a few dollars and buy a black belt from a martial arts supply store, and you can buy a college diploma online. But are those really valuable? Do they have any meaning? The true warrior is dedicated to excellence, not appearances. Think about this.

143

There is nothing so likely to produce peace as to be well prepared to meet the enemy.
George Washington

George Washington, the first President of the United States, knew a fact that it would serve every warrior to realize. Predators look for the easy target. Predators, whether it is the low-level street punk or the serial killer, look for prey that will not put up much of a struggle. They are not out to prove their manhood. They do not want a "fair fight" to test their martial arts skills. All they are interested in is achieving their objective, which is to separate you from your money, your valuables, or even your life.

Knowing this, it is obvious that what George Washington said so many years ago, still applies today. There is nothing so likely to keep a predator from attacking you as your preparedness to meet him with extreme force should he decide to do so. Predators are experts at sizing people up. They can easily identify an easy mark or someone who is probably able to defend themselves on the street. Just as predators in the wild choose to attack the sick or injured, street predators will always choose the easy mark.

Armed with this information, you should present yourself with an aura of confidence when you are out in public. Look people straight in the eye as you walk by. Let them know that you are aware of their presence. Don't walk around with your head down, slumped over, and shuffling along like an old man. Give others the impression that you would be a force to be reckoned with. And, by all means, do not be a pretender; actually be prepared to meet the predator, with the appropriate force, should it come to that.

144

A young man owes respect and gratitude to his father and elders.
Leon Battista Alberti

This statement by Leon Battista Alberti is taken as outdated, ancient hogwash by many young people today. As school teachers, my wife and I see young people who display the complete opposite attitude on a daily basis. They do not seem to have any respect for anyone, their father included. Gratitude is a foreign concept to most young people. They feel that they do not owe anybody anything, whether it is gratitude or respect. This is a sad commentary on our youth and the absence of wisdom in their "education."

Warriors, on the other hand, take respect and gratitude seriously, especially respect for their fathers and elders. Filial duty is one of the traits of the true warrior. He knows that he owes his parents respect, and that it is his duty to take care of his parents when they reach old age. This is not only his duty, but it is also a way of expressing his gratitude for all that his parents have done for him over the years. The true warrior would not even consider neglecting his filial duty.

From what I have observed, it would be very beneficial if the youth of today were brought up in the warrior lifestyle. Many young men today lack the character traits that are a vital part of the warrior lifestyle, traits that could make a huge difference in the lives of young people. Respect and gratitude are only two examples of the character traits which our young people need in their lives. In my opinion, young men and women should be brought up in the warrior lifestyle from the time they are old enough to start learning.

145

To do two things at once is to do neither.
Syrus

To do two things at once is to do neither. In today's world of multi-tasking, this teaching by Syrus may seem ridiculous to many, but what he is saying is true nonetheless. While it is true that you may get things done through multitasking, you are never giving any one thing your total attention, therefore you are actually not doing either to the best of your ability; you are simply, mindlessly breezing through your work at hand, much like someone practicing karate while thinking about paying his bills.

What the warrior needs to remember is that there is power in concentrated thought. Whatever you are doing, be in the moment. Concentrate on that one thing, then go on to something new once you have given that specific task your total attention. By dividing our attention between two or more tasks at the same time, we are not giving any of those things the attention that it deserves. This is when mistakes can and do happen.

This is one reason that one of the most used excuses made for mistakes today is "multi-tasking." Statements such as, "I'm sorry. I was multi-tasking and just wasn't paying attention," are common place today. People think that it makes them sound like hard workers and therefore it is an acceptable excuse for sloppy work. Isn't it better to concentrate on doing one thing at a time, and doing it well? Then you will have no need for excuses or justifying careless mistakes. Do what you do with a sense of excellence.

146

**Given enough time, any man may master the physical.
With enough knowledge, any man may become wise.
It is the true warrior who can master both.**
Tien T'ai

The wisdom in this quote is completely true. Any man can master his physical body given enough time and training. If you train carefully, eat nutritional foods, and keep your body healthy, you can achieve the same amount of physical prowess as the next person. It is up to you how much time you dedicate to your training. Likewise, anyone can become wise if he spends enough time studying and reflecting on true wisdom. Wisdom comes from knowledge and experience, and being wise is a personal decision that someone makes.

Not many people master either of these areas. The common man does not take the time to develop his physical body, and does not see the value in studying to become wise. These things are just not important to him, but according to Tien T'ai teachings, both are important to the true warrior. The warrior must master both his physical side and his intellectual side. Not only should he master these two areas, but he must also keep these areas balanced with the spiritual and emotional parts of his life.

The warrior lifestyle is not the easy road. It is not the path of least resistance, but it is the path of excellence. The true warrior must master a variety of skills, and must keep his life in balance. He should keep his body finely tuned, as well as be a man of wisdom and character. He must stay true to his spiritual beliefs and balance them with the fulfillment of his duties as a warrior. It is essential that he maintains control over his emotions.

147

Pacifists become statistics.
Kevin L. Brett

The warrior doesn't want to fight. He is a peaceful person at heart, with no desire to cause anyone else any pain or harm. Warriors don't enjoy conflict anymore than anyone else, but they know the truth of the above quote from Kevin Brett's book, *The Way of the Martial Artist*. Although he is a peaceful man, he is not a pacifist. A pacifist is someone who refuses to fight, no matter what. The pacifist is the predator's ideal victim. He dreams of finding people who he can prey on and at the same time, they will refuse to fight back.

Those who refuse to fight back do become statistics. They are simply depending on the predator to either not cross their path, or they are depending on the predator's good character and mercy, both of which are risky propositions at best. It is pure gambling to bank on never having to encounter some predator during your lifetime, and when you do, you can be assured that he will not be a man of high character and most likely will show you no mercy.

The warrior understands these facts. Although he is a peace-loving person with no desire for violence, he will fight when he has no acceptable alternatives. He knows that all people are not the same, no matter how politically incorrect this fact may be. Predators do not think like the average person. They have no compulsion about taking advantage of someone's peaceful nature. They only respond to strength and power, not love and idealism. Being a pacifist is a personal choice, and so is being safe and staying alive.

148

A righteous man is cautious in friendship.
The Book of Proverbs

Your choice of possible friends is an important decision. Not everyone should be considered as a good candidate for friendship. Okay, I can already hear you saying, "This guy is a snob!" Well, when it comes to people who I look at as possible true friends, I guess snob would be fitting for me, and it should be fitting for you as well. That is the acronym SNOB, as in "Seeking" "Noble" "Outstanding" "Brethren," not snob as in someone who looks down on others.

You should be selective, very selective, when it comes to people whom you consider people that are worthy of being in your inner circle. The word "friendship" means different things to different people, but to the warrior it takes on a much deeper meaning than that of companion or acquaintance. The warrior takes his real friendships seriously. He is always willing to go to bat for his friends, and he expects his true friends to be willing to have his back when he needs their help.

This relationship is much stronger than that of a simple acquaintance. Therefore, the warrior must be cautious when it comes to friendship. He wants to find friends who are also men of character and honor. There is an old saying that states, there is no friendship among thieves. The same principle applies to men of low character. There is no true friendship with men of low character. It takes a certain amount of character and honor to be a true friend. You have to be trustworthy and sincere, traits which are becoming rare.

149

The surest possession
is real contentment.
Nagarjuna

The man who is content has a feeling of calm satisfaction. If you are content, no matter what situation that you find yourself in, you are relaxed and satisfied with your lot in life, whether it is abundant or meager. This is a great feeling to have. Being content, no matter what, is a choice. It takes some practice to get to that point, but once you have reached the place where you are happy whether you are rich or poor, you have a special possession which nobody can take away from you.

How can the warrior find this kind of peace and contentment in his life? One way is through meditation. Spend time each day in mediation and you will find that you become more peaceful and content with your life. You should also spend time contemplating the things in your life which are really meaningful to you. What really matters in your life? What are the things that are truly important to you? When you reflect on these questions, chances are you will find that the answers have little to do with material possessions.

Being content, like being happy, is a choice that you make. It is totally up to you to decide that you are content with your life. If you find, after meditating and reflecting on the state of your life, that you don't like where you are, or the direction that your life is headed, take the necessary steps to make changes in your life. It is necessary for the warrior to be content with the path that he has chosen to travel. Financial abundance is always nice, but true prosperity is found in contentment.

150

Anger at a petty offense is unworthy of a superior man, but indignation for a great cause is righteous wrath.
Mencius

There is a time and a place for everything, and that includes letting your anger out. I have talked about the need to control your anger, over and over. I spend so much time discussing this one issue because it is an issue that so many people deal with on a daily basis. Being in command of your emotions, whether it is anger, or any other emotion, is vital for the warrior. He simply cannot allow his emotions to dictate his actions – end of story.

But, being in control of your emotions does not mean that you never express your anger. It means that *you choose* when and where you allow your anger to be expressed. *You* are in control, not your emotions. Being angry about small, meaningless aggravations is silly and speaks to your lack of self-control, but as Mencius taught, there is a place and a time to allow your anger to come out of its cage.

Just as with everything else, there is a right way and a wrong way to express your anger, even when you feel it is time to allow your anger to show. You should always remain in control of yourself, even if you are expressing your anger. Don't lose your temper. This is not what is meant by allowing your anger to show. You can express your anger without losing control. Even if the time is right for you to communicate your indignation, you still must do it in the right way. The time is never right for the warrior to lose his temper.

151

It is better to sleep on things beforehand than lie awake about them afterwards.
Baltasar Gracian

Do not rush important decisions. As Baltasar Gracian wrote in, *The Art of Worldly Wisdom*, it is much better to take your time and make an intelligent, informed decision, than to make a quick decision and then lose sleep worrying about your decision for days to come. Most decisions that you have to make do not have to be made immediately. You should seek advice, do some research, meditate on the issue at hand, and then make your decision when you feel comfortable inside your spirit.

Take your time. When you try to rush the decision making process or spend too much time thinking about something, you will find that your mind will become clouded. Do your homework, talk to the appropriate people, meditate, then do something different. Get your mind off of the topic for a while. The reason for this is that it allows you to clear your mind about the subject, and this allows you to listen to what your spirit has to tell you about what you should do. Always listen to your intuition or your spirit.

Another important thing to remember is that, once you have made your decision, do not continually second guess yourself. You took your time, you did your research, you spent time contemplating the different options, and you made the best decision that you could, now be at peace with your decision. Second-guessing your decision only adds stress and worry to your mind. This is especially true when your decision cannot be reversed. You made the best decision that you could, now stand by that decision with confidence.

152

Those who know the
least obey the best.
Farquhar

Warriors of the past have always valued improving their mind. Reading and studying were a part of their routine and they valued knowledge. Just like your counterparts of old, you should also value knowledge. Those without knowledge, as Farquhar states, are easy to control and to take advantage of by those who have knowledge. When knowledge is looked at from this vantage point, you can consider studying and acquiring knowledge of various things, as being part of your self-defense.

Self-defense involves much more than defending yourself physically against some thug, especially in today's society. There are so many ways that people can hurt you today. A physical assault, although the main focus of self-defense for the warrior, is but one way that you can be attacked. Your enemies who are less physical and more educated, will more likely assault you through other means, usually having to do with their knowledge and twisted character.

For this reason, it is vital that you also arm yourself with a well-balanced knowledge of the world. Know your rights and the law so others cannot use your ignorance as a weapon against you. This is important even in a physical confrontation. You must know the law concerning how much force you can legally use, in order to defend yourself against legal prosecution, even though you are in the right. If you lack knowledge, you are putting yourself at risk. Those without knowledge have a hole in their defense. Think about this.

153

Habits change into character.
Ovid

A habit is a regularly repeated behavior pattern that you continue until it becomes a natural part of you. Once a habit has become a part of you, it has become a part of your character. This is why it is important that the warrior keep a close watch over his actions. It seems that it is easier to form bad habits than it is to form good or productive habits. It is definitely easier to lie on the couch and stare mindlessly at the television than it is to force yourself to get up and go workout.

This is why it takes a conscious effort to mold your character into that of a true warrior. As I'm sure you know by now, the warrior lifestyle is not the easiest path to follow. It takes work to follow the path of the warrior. You have to work at developing good habits, habits that will move you closer to your objective of perfecting your character. Anything worth having takes effort and work. If it were easy, everyone would do it, but it is not.

It is like paddling your boat up the river. It takes work to paddle up the river, against the current. Sure, it may be easier to go down the river. That would take very little effort. Simply sit in the boat and do nothing and the current will take you down the river. But the path of the warrior leads upriver, against the current, and you must work hard to get to your objective which lies far upstream. You have to develop the habit of paddling to get where you want to go, other habits will not get you there.

154

Self-knowledge is the beginning of self-improvement.
Spanish Proverb

If you do not know what the problem is, how can you possibly fix it? You must understand something before you can even think about beginning to improve it, this is just common sense. This principle applies to everything whether it is taking care of your lawn or making needed changes in your life to improve your character on the path of the warrior. If you don't have some knowledge about a topic to begin with, what makes you think that you have the knowledge to make it better?

Because of this fact, it is imperative that the warrior take the time to really know who he is, what he believes, and how he thinks. He has to know his weak points and his strong point. He must know if he has a problem with his anger or controlling his temper before he can actually address that problem and learn to take control of his emotions. This is the first step in self-improvement. Take time to get to know yourself and find out what areas of your life need some work.

There are many ways that you can do this. Meditate on what your weak spots are, whether they are mental, physical or emotional, and then focus on strengthening those areas. I have a book out called *Secrets of the Soul*, which is specifically for the purpose of discovering exactly what you believe, how you think, and why you believe what you believe. Reading books that prompt you to examine your life is a good way to learn who you truly are and can give you insight into areas which may be out of sync with the warrior lifestyle. Take the time to know yourself.

155

Intimidation is a state of mind.
Loren W. Christensen

If you find yourself intimidated, you know that you have allowed fear to cloud your thinking. Every man on this earth has certain vulnerable areas on his body that can be attacked, no matter how muscular he is or how mean and tough he appears. Sure that ex-con with evil looking tattoos covering his bulging biceps looks intimidating, but you can't allow yourself to be intimidated by his external appearance. Yes, this is another one of those things that is easier said than done.

Anyway, let's continue with the example of our handsome ex-con. Would you be intimidated by the same guy if he were clean-cut and wearing a pink polo shirt and white Dockers? Not so much? Why not? We are talking about the same muscles on the same body. What makes the difference? The evil looking tattoos? Or maybe the overall appearance which tells us this guy is bad news? While we should pay attention to external signs which can alert us to trouble, we can't let intimidation cloud our mind.

Intimidation and fear can defeat you, and you can't afford to be defeated when your life is on the line. This is where your mental training is important. You cannot allow external appearances to psyche you out. If you do, you are in trouble. You must see yourself as being able to handle any situation, and at the same time be smart enough to know what your limitations are. Loren Christensen goes on to say that, "An opponent… is intimidating only if you allow him to be." Control your mind and intimidation will become a moot point.

156

Honor is a harder master than the law.
Mark Twain

For most people, it is fairly easy to control their behavior and live within the boundaries of the law. The majority of our citizens are law-abiding people who only want to live their lives in peace. And, for those who would rather go against the law, there are incentives in the form of fines and prisons to encourage them to rethink their rebellious attitudes. It is fairly easy for most people to master the law of the land, but when it comes to mastering honor, the same people are at a loss.

Honor is definitely harder to master than the law. One reason for this may be the fact that it is not against the law to be dishonorable, at least not in general. There are things which are perfectly legal, that are completely dishonorable. It seems that most people consider the law of much more importance than their honor. If it isn't illegal, they consider it fair game, no matter how dishonorable it may be. Needless to say, this is not the way of the warrior.

The warrior takes honor seriously. This is another reason that it is harder to live the warrior lifestyle than to live as the average citizen. True warriors have stricter standards to conform to than those of the average person. Their main indicator of whether or not an action is acceptable is based on their sense of honor, not whether or not that action is against the law. The warrior's scale weighs right and wrong, not legal and illegal. He seeks to master honor, not the law. Therefore he lives by a higher standard than most.

157

Thou shalt not be a victim.
Thou shalt not be a perpetrator.
Above all, thou shalt not be a bystander.
Holocaust Museum, Washington, DC

These are all three good rules for the warrior to follow. Don't be a victim, don't be a perpetrator, and don't be a bystander. Warriors rarely have to worry about being the victim or the perpetrator. They train hard in order to prevent themselves from being victims of some violent crime. Self-defense is the basis of the martial arts. Likewise, the warrior would never consider being a perpetrator. His code of honor would never allow him to stoop to that level.

That only leaves the last rule, do not be a bystander. This one is a little trickier for some warriors. Some warriors question whether or not they should get involved in circumstances that are "none of their business." This goes back to the questions of, what is your business and what is not your business? If you are a true warrior, you have a greater responsibility than the average person. You do not have the option of simply refusing to help if someone is getting mugged or assaulted. Helping others is part of your duty and your training.

Being a bystander while you witness someone becoming a victim of a violent crime would be dishonorable. It is sad that anyone would stand by in that situation and not take action, but it is completely unacceptable for the warrior to do so. Part of the warrior lifestyle is service to others. This is one of the reasons that you train. Your martial arts training provides you with the knowledge and skills to keep others safe, and you should use your training to do so.

158

Self-respect is the fruit of discipline; the sense of dignity grows with the ability to say no to oneself.
Abraham J. Heschel

Self-respect is the belief in your own integrity and dignity. This is something that must be cultivated and can only come from the inside. There is no self-respect without self-discipline. Your sense of dignity becomes stronger and stronger as you discipline yourself to live by the standards that you have decided to live by. The lack of standards is one of the main causes of so many people who have no self-respect. When someone does not live by any standards, or lives by low standards, he loses respect for himself.

It is only living in accord with our own personal standards that we feel good about ourselves and start to develop self-respect. You can be very successful, at least externally, and still lack self-respect if you are not living by the standards which you know inside that you should be living by. Self-respect is not something that you can fake. Your conscience knows whether or not you are living up to your standards, and it will not let you off the hook if you have thrown self-discipline to the wind, and lowered your standards.

For the warrior, this means that you develop more and more self-respect as you discipline yourself to live according to your code of honor. The more you discipline yourself to follow the strict standards by which you live, the more concrete your self-respect becomes. You start to respect the fact that you have the fortitude to stand by your beliefs. You know that the warrior lifestyle is one that requires great discipline, and you respect the fact that you have the discipline that it takes to walk this path.

159

A wise man stumbles once over a peg.
Pashto

When you make a mistake, learn from it. Don't make the same mistake repeatedly. If you find that this is exactly what you are doing, whether it is in your martial arts training or in another part of the warrior lifestyle, you know that there is something that you need to change. Doing the same thing over and over again, and expecting different results does not make sense. All actions produce results, and the same actions, done in the same way, will produce the same results.

If the result that a specific action is producing is not what you desire, change the action. As the saying goes, kill the spider and you get rid of the cobweb. When you change the action, you also in effect, change the result. If you do not change the specific action, you will continue to get the same result, time and again. This is what Pashto is saying in this quote. If something is causing you to stumble, do not continue to stumble over it – remove the impediment.

The warrior can relate this to his training in the warrior lifestyle. There are many aspects of the warrior lifestyle that challenge us. Different things can become obstacles in the path of warriorship. When you encounter an obstacle that causes you to stumble, get rid of it. Learn from it and then move on. Do not ignore it, thus having to deal with the same hindrance multiple times. Deal with it once and for all, and get it out of the way. The wise warrior stumbles only once over the same obstacle.

160

The just man is himself his own law.
Catacombs Inscription

I have been accused at times of lacking respect for the law, especially when I write about the true warrior being his own law, and that his law is a higher law than the law of the land. My lack of respect for some of the laws which our "lawmakers" pass each year is a different subject, and probably stems from my time working with several of these "honorable" politicians. Many of the bills that these "leaders" sign into law are as corrupt and misleading as the politicians who sign them – corrupt and dishonest.

Taking this into account, the warrior's own personal "law" is higher than that of the land, higher in character and honor. This is why sages from across the ages from Lao Tzu to Socrates have stated that the just man is his own law. As you know by now, the warrior is a just man, thus it stands to reason that his own personal standards are higher than any corrupt laws or hidden political agendas, which our lawmakers force upon us. His "law" is above reproach, and he refuses to compromise where it is concerned.

The warrior's own "law" is steeped in honor, character and integrity, not personal gain or secret deals made behind closed doors. He can be counted on to do what is right, without fear of the police or government. Even if the thousands of laws which serve to keep lesser men in line were abolished, the true warrior would remain the same. With some minor exceptions, the laws of the land are meaningless to him. He does what is right without regard to laws which are meant to control lesser men. He is himself his own law.

161

Self-discipline is the cornerstone of any endeavor.
Bohdi Sanders

It does not matter what the endeavor is that you aspire to, without self-discipline it will most likely not be successful. Self-discipline is the cornerstone of any successful endeavor, whether it is obtaining a good education or perfecting your martial arts skills. It requires a lot of self-discipline to make yourself get up and workout when all you feel like doing is vegging out on the couch in front of the television and staring mindlessly at that colorful box. Without self-discipline, that is probably what you would do.

Self-discipline is especially important for the warrior. It takes effort to live the lifestyle of the warrior. There is a constant battle raging in the warrior's soul, at least until he has established his code of honor securely in his spirit. The warrior is constantly tempted to set his standards aside and deal with some jerk who just insulted him in a more direct, physical way, but he resists this temptation time and time again. This takes self-discipline, sometimes a lot of self-discipline!

The trick is to continue to discipline yourself until these temptations do not cross your mind when you are dealing with these kinds of people. When you no longer need to discipline yourself in order to walk away from some obnoxious jerk, you know that the warrior lifestyle has become ingrained in your spirit. You naturally do what is right and what is best, and can smile about how the "old" you would have loved to smash this guy's face. With continuous self-discipline, you will reach this point.

162

A wise man fights to win, but he is twice a fool who has no plan for possible defeat.
Louis L'amour

If a situation deteriorates to the point of becoming physical, you should do everything in your power to win the fight and keep yourself and those around you safe. This should go without saying, but you would be surprised at how many people are not prepared to do "whatever it takes." You have to spend time reflecting on what you are willing to do and what you definitely are not willing to do, and what circumstances would trigger certain responses. Are you willing to stick your fingers three inches deep into someone's eye, or completely destroy their knee in order to survive?

Where do you draw the line? Do you draw the line when it comes to fighting to win? Personally, if the situation has reached the point where someone is intent on killing or severely injuring me or those I care about, there are no rules – anything goes. This is a personal decision, and a decision that you should make before you find yourself in this position. You should also be smart enough to have a backup plan in case things don't go your way.

Loren Christensen states that you should never die in training. This means that during your practice, whether it is with a partner or in your visualization time, you should never see yourself dying. I agree with this. Never see yourself getting killed or losing the fight, but you may occasionally see a situation where your technique did not work, and you have to resort to a backup plan. Of course, in the end, your backup plan leaves you victorious over your assailant. Being prepared means being prepared for whatever you may encounter.

163

We must first set our hearts right.
Confucius

It is the nature of the warrior to want to help others with their problems. Warriors train to perfect their martial arts skills in order to be able to keep those around them safe from harm. The warrior studies wisdom and gains knowledge, knowledge which can be used to assist others during their time of need. We want to provide wisdom and instruction for our families, as well as our friends and neighbors. The noble warrior has a heart for others, a heart full of empathy, but before he can help others, he must set his own heart right.

Confucius put it this way, "To put the world right in order, we must first put the nation in order; to put the nation in order, we must first put the family in order; to put the family in order, we must first cultivate our personal life; we must first set our hearts right." The warrior would like to help change the world, but there are many steps that must be taken before he is able to consider doing so. The first priority is setting his own heart right. It all begins with perfecting his own character.

As much as the warrior may want to help others, if his life is a mess and he is not right on the inside, correcting his own shortcomings must be his first priority. You cannot be of much use to others if your own life is not right. This process can be likened to sharing tea with your friends. If your teapot is empty, how can you pour any tea into your friend's cup? You can't share what you don't have. It is an important part of the process for your teapot to be filled before you try to fill others' cups for them. Think about this.

164

From him to whom much is given, much shall be expected.
Jesus

This admonition from Jesus is one that every true warrior should constantly be mindful of throughout his life. The warrior has been given much and therefore it is his responsibility to use what he has been given. He has been given special training concerning the martial arts and self-defense, which very few others have had access to. He has studied and understands the importance of character, integrity and honor. He walks in the ways of wisdom and has refined his mind and his spirit.

The warrior knows the importance of knowledge, and has worked to obtain a certain level of understanding and awareness that others may lack. These men of valor see things in a different way than the ordinary person; they have developed insights which elude the common man. His training has afforded him much, and thus much is to be expected of him. It has been this way throughout the ages. The true warrior is what Confucius called "the superior man," and as such he has greater duties than the average man.

This is what is expected on the warrior's path. You have been given much in the way of training and knowledge, and as a true warrior you should use what you have been given to help those around you. You may not be in a position to help others financially, but you can use your training and knowledge to help them in other ways. Much has been given to you, now it is up to you to use what you have been given in the correct way. This attitude of service and character is what separates the true warrior from the mere fighter.

Bushido
The Way of the Warrior

I see things through different eyes.
I see a bigger picture when others see grey skies.
Though many can't conceive it, I stand…facing the wind.
My bravery not from fighting, but from my strength within.
I am a warrior; I'll walk the extra mile.
Not because I have to, but because it's worth my while.
I know that I am different when I stand on a crowded street.
I know the fullness of winning; I've tasted the cup of defeat.
I am a warrior; they say I walk with ease.
Though trained for bodily harm, my intentions are for peace.
The world may come and go, but a different path I'll choose.
A path I will not stray from, no matter win or lose.

(Anonymous)

Afterword

Thank you for your purchase of *The Warrior Lifestyle*. I hope that you found the wisdom contained within to be useful in your life and for your goals as you travel along the path of the warrior. This is the final book of the three volume *Warrior Wisdom Series*. Taken together, the books in the *Warrior Wisdom Series* offer readers valuable insights into the warrior lifestyle, as well as the motivation needed to continue to live a life of excellence in a world of compromise. This is the life of warriorhood.

You should continue to refer back to, not only this book, but also to *Warrior Wisdom: Ageless Wisdom for the Modern Warrior*, *Warrior Wisdom: The Heart and Soul of Bushido*, and *Modern Bushido*, on a regular basis to keep your mind focused on the traits which make someone a true warrior in life. Our lives are so hectic and busy in today's world that it is easy to forget the traits which we strive to live by on the path of the warrior. Daily reading and meditation on these character traits, goals, and objectives help keep one focused and also help in preventing one from forgetting the importance of his or her commitment to excellence.

When judging whether or not a book is one in which I find to be worthwhile, I continue to refer back to the wise words by Theodore Parker which state, "The books that help you most are those which make you think the most." I hope that you find that *The Warrior Lifestyle*, as well as the other two books in the *Warrior Wisdom Series*, have sincerely made you think and helped you on your personal journey to live the life of the warrior – the path of the true human being.

I would love to hear your feedback on *Warrior Wisdom*. What do you feel about what you have read? Did you find it helpful? Please send your comments on this, or any of the books in the *Warrior Wisdom* series, to me. You may contact me by e-mail at: WarriorWisdom@comcast.net, please put "Feedback" in the heading.

Live with honor!

Bohdi SandersPhD

Appendix

a'Kempis, Thomas – (1380 –1471), was a late Medieval Catholic
monk and author of *The Imitation of Christ.*

Aesop – 6ᵗʰ century Greek author of *Aesop's Fables.*

Alberti, Leon Battista – (1404 –1472), was an Italian author, artist,
architect, poet, priest, linguist, philosopher, and cryptographer,

Aristotle – (384 BC–322 BC), Greek philosopher, a student of Plato
and teacher of Alexander the Great.

Aurelius, Marcus – (121–180), was Roman Emperor from 161 to his
death in 180. He was the last of the "Five Good Emperors",
and is also considered one of the most important Stoic
philosophers.

Baba, Sai – South Indian guru, religious leader, orator.

Bodhidharma – Buddhist monk traditionally
credited as the bring martial arts to China.

Book of Proverbs, The – one of the books of the Bible, called the
book of wisdom.

Brett, Kevin L. – martial artist and author of *The Way of the Martial
Artist.*

Buddha – (563 BCE– 483 BC), spiritual teacher from ancient India
and the founder of Buddhism.

Burrese, Alain – martial artist and author of *Hard Won Wisdom from
The School of Hard Knocks.*

Cervantes, Miguel de – (1547–1616), was a Spanish novelist, poet, painter and playwright. Cervantes is one of the most important and influential people in literature and the author of the novel *Don Quixote.*

Christensen, Loren – martial artist and author of over 30 books, most on martial arts.

Churchill, Winston – (1874 –1965), was a British politician known chiefly for his leadership of the United Kingdom during World War II.

Chung Yung – is both a concept and one of the books of Neo Confucian teachings.

Code of the Samurai, The – a modern translation of the Bushido Shoshinshu.

Confucius – (551 BC–479 BC), Chinese thinker and social philosopher, whose teachings and philosophy have deeply influenced Chinese, Korean, Japanese, and Vietnamese thought and life. .

Dekanawidah – The Great Peacemaker was, along with Hiawatha, the traditional founder of the Haudenosaunee (commonly called the *Iroquois*) Confederacy.

Demeere, Wim – martial artist and author of *The Fighter's Body.*

Democritus – (460 BC–370 BC), was a pre-Socratic Greek philosopher.

Deshimaru, Taisen – (1914–1982), Japanese Soto Zen Buddhist teacher. Born in the Saga Prefecture of Kyushu, Deshimaru was raised by his grandfather, a former Samurai before the Meiji Revolution.

Dogen – (1200–1253), Japanese Zen Buddhist teacher born in Kyôto, and the founder of the Sôtô school of Zen in Japan.

Einstein, Albert – (1879 –1955), was a German-American physicist. He is best known for his special and general theories of relativity, but contributed in other areas of physics.

Eliot, T. S. – (1888–1965), was an American-born English poet, dramatist and literary critic.

Emerson, Ralph Waldo – (1803–1882), American essayist, philosopher, poet, and leader of the Transcendentalist movement in the early 19th century.

Erasmus, Desiderius – (1466/1469 –1536), was a Dutch Renaissance Humanist and Catholic Christian theologian.

Euripides – (480 BC–406 BC), was the last of the three great tragedians of classical Athens.

Farquhar – (1677 –1707), was an Irish dramatist.

Foch, Marshall Ferdinand – (1851–1929), was a French soldier, military theorist, and writer.

Franklin, Benjamin – (1706 –1790), was an American inventor, journalist, printer, diplomat, and statesman.

Frederick, Carl – a German-American professor and political theorist.

Funakoshi, Gichin – (1868–1957), founder of Shotokan karate and is attributed as being the "father of modern karate."

Furuya, Kensho – martial artist, chief instructor of the Aikido Center in Los Angeles.

Gandhi – (1869–1948), was a major political and spiritual leader of India and the Indian independence movement.

Goethe, Johann Wolfgang von – (1749–1832), was a German novelist, dramatist, poet, humanist, scientist, and philosopher.

Gracian, Baltasar – (1601–1658), Spanish Baroque prose writer.

Guicciardini, Francesco – (1483–1540), Italian historian and statesman. He is considered one of the major political writers of the Italian Renaissance.

Hadith – oral traditions relating to the words and deeds of Muhammad.

Hatsumi, Masaaki – founder and current head of the Bujinkan Dojo martial arts organization.

Havamal, The – Ancient Viking text.

Hawk – Native American warrior.

Herbert, George – (1593–1633), was a Welsh poet, orator and priest.

Herodotus – (484 BC–425 BC), was a historian, known for his writings on the conflict between Greece and Persia.

Heschel, Abraham J. – (1907–1972), was a Warsaw-born American rabbi and one of the leading Jewish theologians.

Holmes, Oliver Wendell – (1841–1935), was an American jurist who served on the Supreme Court of the United States.

Hurwitt, Samuel J. – American writer.

Jesus – (2 BC–36 AD), also known as Jesus Christ, is the central figure of Christianity and is revered by most Christian churches as the Son of God.

Jones, Tony L. – SWAT officer and author of over 9 books.

Jung, Carl – (1875–1961), was a Swiss psychiatrist, an influential thinker and the founder of Analytical psychology.

Kane, Lawrence A. – martial artist and author of *The Little Black Book Of Violence*.

L'amour, Louis – (1908–1988), was an American author.

La Rochefoucauld – (1613–1680), was a noted French author of *Maxims and Reflections*, as well as an example of the accomplished 17th-century nobleman.

Lee, Bruce – (1940–1973), American-born martial artist, philosopher, instructor, martial arts actor and the founder of the Jeet Kune Do martial arts system.

Lieh Tzu – 4th century Taoist scripture.

Lord Chesterfield – (1694–1773), was a British statesman.

MacArthur, Douglas – (1880–1964), was an American general, United Nations general and Field Marshal of the Philippine Army.

Mencius – (372BC–289 BC), was a Chinese philosopher who was arguably the most famous Confucian after Confucius himself.

Miyagi, Gojun – Japanese martial artist.

Montaigne, Michel – (1533–1592), one of the most influential writers of The French Renaissance.

Morgan, Forrest E. – martial artist and author of *Living the Martial Way*.

Morihei, Ueshiba – (1883–1969) was a famous martial artist and founder of the Japanese martial art of Aikido.

Morris, Glenn – martial artist, ninja master, and author.

Musashi, Miyamoto – (1584–1645), Japanese swordsman famed for his duels and distinctive style.

Nagarjuna – (150–250), Indian philosopher, the founder of the Madhyamaka (Middle Path) school of Mahâyâna Buddhism, and arguably the most influential Buddhist thinker after Gautama Buddha himself.

Nagauji, Hojo – chief of the Kyoto agency in the 1300's.

Ohiyesa – (1858 –1939), was a Native American author, physician and reformer.

Otsuka, Hironori – (1892–1982), created the Wadô-ryû style of karate. He was the first Grand Master of Wadô-ryû karate.

Ovid – (43 BC–17 AD), Publius Ovidius Naso, Roman poet.

Paine, Thomas – (1737–1809), was a British pamphleteer, revolutionary, radical, inventor, and intellectual. He wrote *Common Sense* in 1776.

Pandit, Sakya – (1182–1251), Tibetan scholar.

Paul, The Apostle – the most notable of early Christian missionaries.

Phaedrus – (15 BC–AD 50) was a Roman fabulist.

Pindar – (522 BC–443 BC), was an Ancient Greek lyric poet.

Proust, Marcel – (1871–1922), was a French novelist, essayist and critic.

Pulitzer, Joseph – (1847–1911), was a Hungarian-American publisher Best known for posthumously establishing the Pulitzer Prizes.

Ramakrishna – (1836–1886), a famous mystic of 19th century India.

Reeves, Mike – martial artist and author of *Ultimate Combat Conditioning for the Street Warrior*.

Saint Thomas of Aquinas – (1225–1274), was a priest of the Roman Catholic Church in the Dominican Order from Italy, and an immensely influential philosopher and theologian.

Seneca – (54 BC–39 AD), was a Roman rhetorician and writer.

Shakespeare, William – (1564–1616), English poet and playwright, widely regarded as the greatest writer in the English language.

Shaw, Scott – martial artist and author of *The Warrior is Silent*.

Shelley, Percy Bysshe – (1792–1822), was one of the major English Romantic poets and is among the finest lyric poets in the English language.

Sockman, Ralph W. – (1889–1970), was the senior pastor of Christ Church in New York.

Sophocles – (496 BC–406 BC), was an ancient Greek playwright, dramatist, priest, and politician of Athens.

Sprague, Martina – author of *The Laws of Physics for Martial Artists*.

Stevenson, Robert Louis – (1850–1894), was a Scottish novelist, poet, essayist and travel writer.

Strabo – (63/64 BC–AD 24), was a Greek historian, geographer and philosopher.

Syrus – Roman philosopher.

T'ai, Tian – one of the important sects of Buddhism in China, Korea and Japan, also called the Lotus School because of its emphasis on the Lotus Sutra.

Tabata, Kazumi – martial artist and author of *Secret Tactics*.

Tiruvalluvar – 2nd century BC Tamil poet who wrote the Thirukkural, a well-known ethical work in Tamil literature.

Twain, Mark – (1835–1910), was an American author and humorist.

Tzu, Chuang – (369 BC–286 BC), literally *Master Zhuang*, was a Chinese philosopher, who is supposed to have lived during the Warring States Period.

Tzu, Lao – 6th century BC philosopher of ancient China and is a central figure in Taoism.

Tzu, Sun – (544 BC– 496 BC), the author of *The Art of War*, an immensely influential ancient Chinese book on military strategy.

Voltaire – (1694– 1778), was a French writer, deist and philosopher.

Washington, George – (1732– 1799), the first President of the United States, after leading the Continental Army to victory over the Kingdom of Great Britain in the American Revolutionary War (1775–1783).

Zeno the Stoic – (334 BC– 262 BC), was a Greek philosopher, Zeno was the founder of the Stoic school of philosophy which he taught in Athens.

Index

A

a'Kempis, Thomas, 169
acquaintance, 60, 62, 148
action, iii, ix, x, 5, 6, 8, 9, 13, 30, 34, 36,
    43, 44, 45, 47, 49, 65, 66, 68, 84, 86,
    94, 100, 103, 108, 110, 113, 114, 129,
    156, 157, 159
actions, x, xi, xiii, 8, 9, 17, 18, 21, 22, 27,
    28, 33, 34, 38, 43, 49, 51, 52, 53, 58,
    63, 65, 68, 72, 77, 84, 85, 87, 89, 91,
    93, 98, 102, 104, 108, 110, 114, 121,
    124, 125, 129, 131, 135, 140, 150, 153,
    159
adrenaline, 8, 17, 96, 124, 132
Aesop, iii, 6, 85, 169
Alain Burrese, i, 82
Alberti, Leon Battista, 169
anger, x, 8, 17, 36, 54, 81, 84, 86, 96, 100,
    114, 121, 124, 125, 135, 137, 150, 154
apathy, 20
Aristotle, iv, 98, 140, 169
attitude, 8, 10, 24, 46, 48, 76, 100, 105,
    131, 144, 164
Aurelius, Marcus, 169
awareness, 2, 13, 135, 138, 164
Awareness, 112

B

Baba, Sai, 169
balance, iv, xiv, 23, 70, 117, 120, 133, 146
Baltasar Gracian, 12, 39, 109, 139, 151
be prepared, 20, 23, 96, 103, 107, 136,
    138, 143
Benjamin Franklin, iv, 4, 51
Bias, 55
Bodhidharma, 38, 169
Bohdi Sanders, 3, ii, iii, iv, v, vi, vii, viii, ix,
    xiv, 21, 65, 161, 184
Book of Proverbs, 148, 169
Bruce Lee, iv, 97, 101
Buddha, iii, 67, 134, 169, 173

C

calm mind, 8
careless, 57, 68, 76, 81, 145
Carelessness, 48
Carl Frederick, 40
Cervantes, vii, 31, 170
character, iv, xi, xii, xiii, xiv, 5, 7, 11, 22,
    25, 27, 31, 32, 33, 35, 44, 52, 61, 70,
    74, 77, 78, 79, 80, 87, 88, 89, 90, 91,
    92, 94, 95, 98, 102, 103, 104, 108, 110,
    113, 116, 117, 123, 129, 130, 134, 136,
    140, 141, 144, 146, 147, 148, 152, 153,
    154, 160, 163, 164, 167, 184
Charles Ward, v
Charlie Ward, i
Chief Joseph, 10
Chung Yung, 92, 170
Churchill, iii, iv, 5, 170
Cicero, 130
code of conduct, 52
code of honor, xii, xiii, 18, 32, 33, 45, 61,
    78, 79
Code of the Samurai, 134, 170
compromise, 15, 33, 35, 37, 45, 53, 83,
    90, 95, 160, 167
Confucius, iii, iv, 11, 15, 57, 77, 87, 134,
    163, 164, 170, 173
conscience, iii, 46, 53, 141, 158
consequence, 38
consequences, 22, 28, 34, 38, 57, 84, 98,
    108, 114, 125, 127, 128, 140
control, ix, 6, 8, 17, 29, 36, 38, 39, 42, 43,
    54, 61, 67, 68, 69, 70, 99, 100, 104,
    107, 108, 121, 124, 131, 132, 135, 139,
    140, 146, 150, 152, 154, 156, 160
convictions, 37, 92
courage, iii, 9, 27, 29, 30, 35, 92, 102, 104,
    126
courageous, 9, 102
courtesy, 60
cowardly, 9, 141

D

Dave Grossman, 42
death, x, 9, 12, 17, 24, 28, 73, 97, 130, 169
decisions, 7, 9, 18, 27, 28, 29, 38, 58, 79, 121, 127, 131, 151
dedication, xiv, 81, 82, 142
Dedication, 142
defeat, 19, 21, 25, 61, 65, 73, 81, 86, 88, 101, 107, 118, 124, 135, 155, 162, 165
Defeat, 73
Dekanawidah, 54, 170
Democritus, 140, 170
Deshimaru, 14, 170
discernment, 22
discipline, xiv, 32, 107, 108, 113, 120, 127, 133, 158, 161
dishonorable, 22, 45, 47, 90, 94, 129, 139, 140, 156, 157
Dogen, 3, 170
Douglas MacArthur, iv, 24
duty, iii, xiii, 9, 16, 22, 30, 42, 78, 81, 85, 131, 141, 144, 157

E

Einstein, 20, 79, 171
Eliot, 111, 171
Emerson, 110, 171
emotions, 6, 17, 29, 36, 38, 43, 54, 67, 100, 105, 121, 125, 132, 146, 150, 154
enemy, xii, 4, 5, 8, 13, 14, 17, 19, 21, 24, 48, 60, 61, 65, 68, 76, 88, 101, 118, 128, 135, 137, 143
Erasmus, 73, 171
ethical standards, 35
Euripides, 29, 171
evil, 20, 27, 42, 56, 58, 109, 141, 155
excellence, xii, xiv, 28, 44, 46, 58, 59, 79, 87, 95, 113, 115, 116, 120, 123, 141, 142, 145, 146, 167
experience, vii, xii, 26, 31, 132, 146

F

F. J. Chu, i, vii
family, xi, 16, 55, 56, 58, 62, 69, 117, 163
Farquhar, 152, 171
fear, 2, 6, 9, 19, 20, 36, 54, 72, 104, 126, 155, 160

fight, xii, 9, 12, 14, 18, 21, 24, 25, 29, 62, 72, 73, 78, 82, 88, 96, 101, 104, 126, 136, 143, 147, 162
fighting, ix, x, xiii, 9, 12, 21, 24, 25, 30, 73, 78, 96, 101, 125, 137, 162, 165
first attack, 13, 65
Foch, 49, 171
Focus, 19, 51, 64, 77, 112
forgive, 4, 77
forgiving, 4
Forrest Morgan, 125
Frederick, 171
friend, i, v, 14, 16, 60, 62, 71, 148, 163
friends, 60, 62, 71, 80, 103, 117, 148, 163
friendship, 1, 16, 60, 71, 80, 148
Furuya, 136, 171

G

Gandhi, 108, 130, 171
Generosity, 30
gentleman, 119
George Herbert, 125
George Washington, iii, 56, 143
Gichin Funakoshi, 25, 33, 82, 95
goal, 15, 17, 24, 25, 49, 78, 79, 88, 95, 108, 113, 137
Goethe, 68, 171
Gojun Miyagi, 88
Golden Rule, 52
Gracian, 12, 171
Guicciardini, 13, 46, 58, 76, 172

H

habit, 28, 67, 88, 134, 153
Hadith, 47, 111, 172
Havamal, 30, 74, 172
Hawk, 126, 172
Herodotus, 93, 172
Heschel, 158, 172
higher law, 34, 90, 160
honesty, 41
honor, i, iii, iv, x, xii, xiii, xiv, 5, 7, 11, 15, 18, 21, 25, 26, 27, 30, 32, 33, 35, 38, 40, 41, 44, 45, 49, 52, 53, 58, 59, 61, 64, 67, 70, 75, 77, 78, 79, 80, 83, 85, 87, 89, 90, 91, 92, 94, 103, 105, 110, 116, 123, 129, 130, 136, 140, 141, 148, 156, 157, 158, 160, 161, 164, 167, 184

Hui Neng, 3
Hurwitt, 121, 172

I

ideals, xiv, 7, 29, 78, 79, 123
ideals of the warrior, xiv, 7
inner spirit, 3
insight, vii, xii, 11, 31, 38, 100, 102, 154
instructors, 21
integrity, iv, xiv, 7, 27, 33, 38, 41, 44, 52,
    61, 74, 77, 78, 79, 80, 83, 85, 89, 91,
    92, 103, 116, 130, 140, 141, 158, 160,
    164, 184
intention, 6, 18, 94, 102, 129
intentions, 2, 6, 27, 94, 102, 129, 140, 165
intuition, 3, 65, 67, 75, 151

J

Jesus, iii, iv, 164, 172
Jones, 86, 172
judgment, 22, 84
Jung, 37, 172
just man, 25, 106, 160
justice, 20, 33, 91, 106

K

karate, 13, 25, 65, 97, 145, 171, 174
karma, 4, 38, 63, 68
Kevin Brett, i, iii, 147
kind word, 81
knowledge, v, vi, xii, xiii, 10, 11, 19, 111,
    119, 125, 133, 139, 146, 152, 154, 157,
    163, 164
Kris Wilder, i, viii

L

L'amour, Louis, 172
La Rochefoucauld, 7, 100, 173
Lao Tzu, iii, iv, 19, 44, 99, 160
law of cause and effect, 38
law of reciprocity, 63
Lawrence Kane, 137
Leon Battista Alberti, 144
Lieh Tzu, 80, 173
life of excellence, xii, 79, 85, 167

lifestyle of excellence, xiv
limits, x, 19, 26
Lord Chesterfield, 119, 173
Loren Christensen, iv, 72, 123, 155, 162
Loren W. Christensen, i, xi, 123, 155

M

man of honor, 32, 33, 58
man of wisdom, 6
Marcel Proust, 115
Marcus Aurelius, vii, 34, 109, 113, 131
Mark Twain, iv, 104, 156
martial arts, ii, iv, v, ix, x, xii, xiii, 3, 5, 11,
    12, 14, 21, 23, 25, 36, 42, 50, 61, 78,
    80, 81, 82, 96, 97, 101, 103, 112, 117,
    118, 119, 120, 126, 133, 136, 138, 139,
    142, 143, 157, 159, 161, 163, 164, 169,
    170, 172, 173
Martina Sprague, 129
Masaaki Hatsumi, 4, 22
meditating, 15, 78, 149
meditation, ii, 8, 19, 23, 36, 67, 70, 92,
    133, 139, 149, 167
Mencius, 150, 173
mind, ii, iv, xi, xiii, 1, 2, 8, 23, 28, 29, 36,
    41, 46, 47, 48, 51, 54, 61, 65, 67, 72,
    73, 76, 79, 81, 84, 99, 102, 105, 108,
    119, 120, 124, 125, 126, 128, 130, 132,
    134, 135, 140, 151, 152, 155, 161, 164,
    167
mistakes, 14, 17, 27, 28, 31, 77, 93, 103,
    114, 145
moderation, 35
Montaigne, 78, 173
Morihei Ueshiba, 1
Morris, 25, 118, 173
motives, 40
Musashi, iv, 75, 120, 173

N

Nagarjuna, 61, 124, 149, 173
Nagauji, 87, 173
Native American, 10, 172, 174
negative emotions, 54
noble, 74, 108, 163

O

obligation, 184
Ohiyesa, 70, 174
Oliver Wendell Holmes, 94
one pointed focus, 112
Otsuka, 138, 174
Ovid, 153, 174

P

Pandit, 28, 174
path of the warrior, vii, xiv, 4, 25, 44, 53,
    88, 111, 123, 129, 153, 154, 167
patient, 95
peace, xiii, 46, 53, 76, 139, 143, 147, 149,
    151, 156, 165
perfection of character, xii, 44, 79, 95, 108
personal information, 14, 68, 122
Phaedrus, 41, 174
physical encounter, 9, 50
physical threat, 13
Pindar, 114, 174
predators, 42, 73, 143
Predators, 143, 147
present moment, xiv, 107, 112, 114
pride, 6, 9, 29, 49
principle, 17, 35, 49, 63, 72, 89, 114, 132,
    148, 154
principles, iii, xiv, 7, 11, 15, 29, 30, 35, 37,
    40, 41, 45, 58, 67, 123
promise, 90
promises, 90
protect, xiii, 21, 22, 34, 42, 61, 74, 82, 99,
    139
Pulitzer, 105, 174

R

Ramakrishna, 52, 174
rational thought, 8, 17, 29, 54, 104, 105,
    121, 124, 126, 135
Reeves, 142, 174
reputation, xiii, 10, 11, 57, 61, 74, 81, 89
respect, 5, 16, 59, 79, 90, 100, 144, 158,
    160
responsibility, 27, 43, 84, 98, 157, 164

S

sages, 11, 17, 30, 31, 39, 52, 58, 64, 67,
    71, 79, 81, 98, 111, 124, 125, 130, 160
Sai Baba, 77, 132
Saint Thomas of Aquinas, 71, 174
Samuel Coleridge, 18
samurai, 11, 87, 134
Secrets of the Soul, ii, 154
self-control, 8, 43, 108, 150
self-defense, iv, xii, 36, 61, 82, 136, 152,
    164
self-discipline, xiv, 107, 108, 113, 125,
    135, 158, 161
self-sufficient, 69
Seneca, iii, 11, 64, 174
service, iii, xiv, 16, 64, 105, 110, 116, 157,
    164
Shakespeare, 9, 174
Shaw, 135, 175
Shelley, 175
Shotokan, ii, 171
Sockman, 103, 175
Sophocles, 27, 175
speaking, 10, 14, 44, 51, 78, 84, 86, 88
speech, 10, 38, 39, 57, 68, 70, 75, 81, 114,
    121
standards, xii, xiv, 15, 21, 33, 34, 52, 53,
    56, 58, 67, 70, 77, 79, 87, 89, 91, 106,
    110, 113, 123, 156, 158, 160, 161
Stevenson, 116, 175
Strabo, 16, 175
stress, 4, 6, 23, 81, 121, 151
Sun Tzu, iii, iv, ix, 8, 19, 23, 96, 101
superior man, 16, 21, 27, 77, 87, 92, 150,
    164
Superior men, 59
Syrus, 145, 175

T

Tabata, 128, 175
temper, x, xi, 6, 35, 100, 124, 150, 154
The Art of War, 176
The Code of the Samurai, 130
think rationally, 8, 17, 23, 29, 99, 105,
    124, 125, 132, 135
Thomas a'Kempis, 43
Thomas Paine, iii, 35, 53

thoughts, xiv, 4, 6, 8, 10, 29, 34, 37, 38, 67, 75, 99, 108, 112, 129, 131, 139, 140

Tien T'ai, 146

Tiruvalluvar, x, 45, 60, 91, 175

train, iv, vii, 1, 23, 36, 103, 120, 127, 138, 139, 146, 157, 163

training, xii, xiii, 5, 8, 23, 26, 36, 50, 65, 70, 72, 76, 82, 92, 105, 107, 127, 133, 136, 138, 139, 146, 155, 157, 159, 162, 164

true warrior, xii, xiii, xiv, 1, 11, 25, 27, 33, 35, 39, 44, 47, 49, 52, 59, 64, 67, 77, 78, 92, 105, 106, 108, 123, 136, 139, 141, 142, 144, 146, 153, 157, 160, 164, 167

True warriors, xiv, 7, 156

U

U. S. Martial Arts Hall of Fame, ii

ultimate objective, 9, 25, 95, 137

V

victory, i, xii, 19, 21, 24, 25, 62, 88, 96, 124, 137, 176

virtue, 30, 98

virtues, 23, 30, 32

Visualization, 72

visualizing, 139

Voltaire, 95, 176

W

Warrior code, 34

warrior lifestyle, v, xii, xiv, 1, 7, 13, 16, 19, 22, 34, 44, 47, 52, 58, 67, 78, 79, 81, 85, 108, 110, 111, 112, 113, 115, 123, 141, 144, 146, 153, 154, 156, 157, 158, 159, 161, 167, 184

warriorhood, ix, 134, 167

warriorship, xii, 120, 159

way of the warrior, 1, 27, 76, 131, 141, 156

Wim Demeere, i, vi, 42

wisdom, ii, iii, iv, vi, vii, viii, xi, xiii, 1, 6, 7, 9, 10, 11, 16, 30, 31, 39, 44, 52, 59, 62, 63, 64, 85, 100, 119, 124, 127, 134, 144, 146, 163, 164, 167, 169, 184

Wisdom, 184

Wisdom Warrior, 184

wise man, 4, 6, 11, 15, 16, 28, 31, 39, 57, 80, 99, 100, 159, 162

words, vii, 10, 11, 31, 39, 57, 68, 72, 81, 86, 90, 109, 110, 114, 167, 172

Z

Zen, vi, 3, 112, 115, 119, 170

Zeno the Stoic, 106, 176

Other Titles by Bohdi Sanders

Character! Honor! Integrity! Are these traits that guide your life and actions? *Warrior Wisdom: Ageless Wisdom for the Modern Warrior* focuses on how to live your life with character, honor and integrity. This book is highly acclaimed, has won multiple awards and is endorsed by some of the biggest names in martial arts and the world of self-help. *Warrior Wisdom* is filled with wise quotes and useful information for anyone who strives to live a life of excellence. This book will help you live your life to the fullest!

Warrior is the second book in the *Warrior Wisdom Series*. Wisdom, life-changing quotes, and entertaining, practical commentaries fill every page. This series has been recognized by four martial arts hall of fame organizations for its inspirational and motivational qualities. The ancient and modern wisdom in this book will definitely help you improve your life and bring meaning to each and every day. The USMAA Hall of Fame awarded Dr. Sanders with Inspiration of the Year for this series!

Secrets of the Soul is a guide to uncovering your deeply hiden beliefs. This delightful book provides over 1,150 probing questions which guide you to a thorough understanding of who you are and what you believe. Take this unbelievably entertaining journey to a much deeper place of self-awareness. Where do your beliefs come from? Do you really know exactly what you believe and why you believe it? You will after reading *Secrets of the Soul*. This book will help you uncover your true beliefs!

Other Titles by Bohdi Sanders

Wisdom of the Elders is a unique, one-of-a-kind quote book. This book is filled with quotes that focus on living life to the fullest with honor, character, and integrity. Honored by the USA Book News with a 1st place award for Best Books of the Year in 2010, this book is a guide for life. *Wisdom of the Elders* contains over 4,800 quotes, all which lead the reader to a life of excellence. If you enjoy quotes, wisdom, and knowledge, you will love this book. This is truly the ultimate quote book for those searching for wisdom!

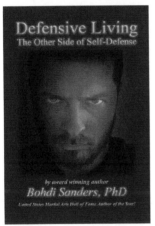

Defensive Living takes the reader deep into the minds of nine of the most revered masters of worldly wisdom. It reveals valuable insights concerning human nature from some of the greatest minds the world has ever known, such as Sun Tzu, Gracian, Goethe, and others. *Defensive Living* presents invaluable lessons for living and advice for avoiding the many pitfalls of human relationships. This is an invaluable and entertaining guidebook for living a successful and rewarding life!

Modern Bushido is all about living a life of excellence. This book covers 30 essential traits that will change your life. *Modern Bushido* expands on the standards and principles needed for a life of excellence, and applies them directly to life in today's world. Readers will be motivated and inspired by the straightforward wisdom in this enlightening book. If you want to live a life of excellence, this book is for you! This is a must read for every martial artist and anyone who seeks to live life as it is meant to be lived.

Looking for More Wisdom?

If you are interested in living the warrior lifestyle or simply in living a life of character, integrity and honor you will enjoy The Wisdom Warrior website and newsletter. The Wisdom Warrior website contains dozens of articles, useful links, and news for those seeking to live the warrior lifestyle.

The newsletter is also a valuable resource. Each edition of The Wisdom Warrior Newsletter is packed with motivating quotes, articles, and information which everyone will find useful in their journey to perfect their character and live the life which they were meant to live.

The Wisdom Warrior Newsletter is a newsletter sent directly to your email account and is absolutely FREE! There is no cost or obligation to you whatsoever. You will also receive the current news updates and new articles by Dr. Bohdi Sanders as soon as they are available. Your email address is never shared with anyone else.

All you need to do to start receiving this valuable and informative newsletter is to go to the Wisdom Warrior website and simply sign up. It is that simple! You will find The Wisdom Warrior website at:

www.TheWisdomWarrior.com

Also, be sure to find posts by Dr. Sanders on Facebook. Dr. Sanders posts enlightening commentaries, photographs, and quotes throughout the week on his Facebook pages. You can find them at:

www.facebook.com/The.Warrior.Lifestyle

www.facebook.com/EldersWisdom

www.facebook.com/bohdi.sanders

Don't miss the opportunity to receive tons of FREE wisdom, enlightening posts, interesting articles, and intriguing photographs on The Wisdom Warrior website and on Dr. Sanders' Facebook pages.

Sign Up Today!

Made in the USA
San Bernardino, CA
25 April 2014